Praise for *The Luckiest Man*

"This is a beautiful, tender, courageous, and inspiring story. Honestly, I take my shoes off. John is a hero of mine. I know you will love this book!"

—JOHN ELDREDGE, FOUNDER OF RANSOMED HEART MINISTRIES
AND AUTHOR OF *WILD AT HEART* AND *ALL THINGS NEW*

"The life and testimony of John Paine has been a tool in the hands of God. John's grace and friendship in the continuing debilitation of ALS has allowed us to watch from the sidelines how and what God has taught him. What God has miraculously shaped in him is a disciple's heart stripped of all unproductive distractions from this earthly life. This book will be key to the extended legacy of a man who has learned to walk with God like few others."

—DR. MARK L. BAILEY, PRESIDENT OF DALLAS
THEOLOGICAL SEMINARY, DALLAS, TX

"I cannot remember the last time God met me so deeply and spoke to me so profoundly through the pages of a book. John Paine's journey of the heart inspired me, convicted me, and surprised and delighted me with multiple fresh encounters of God's great love for me. Thank you, John! Read it, then read it again, then pass it on to someone you love."

—CHIP INGRAM, SENIOR PASTOR OF VENTURE CHRISTIAN
CHURCH IN SILICON VALLEY, CALIFORNIA, CEO AND FOUNDER
OF LIVING ON THE EDGE, AND AUTHOR OF *THE REAL GOD*

"As John Paine, my friend and mentor since his diagnosis, has traveled a road far more challenging than most, he knows God and the ways of God in amazing depth. Put *The Luckiest Man at* the top of your must-read list."

—DON STEPHENS, FOUNDER AND PRESIDENT OF MERCY SHIPS

"Many books say something. Fewer books have something to say. John Paine has captured the essence of life."

—MIKE DOWNEY, FOUNDER OF STRATEGIC IMPACT INTERNATIONAL

"John Paine has been a friend and mentor to me, graciously inviting me into relationship and sharing his walk with God on many occasions. Every time we met I have felt comforted, encouraged, and challenged. As I read through *The Luckiest Man* I felt my heart desiring to know God more intimately, to experience his love more deeply and to trust him more fully. John's story of unexpected joy in his breaking is a fresh invitation into relationship with God our Father."

—NEIL TOMBA, SENIOR PASTOR OF NORTHWEST BIBLE CHURCH, DALLAS, TX

"In *The Luckiest Man* you take a journey into John's life. John oozes with the sweetness of Jesus, not the irritation of the disease, because he has learned the secret of intimacy with God. He shares many truths and nuggets of how we can also practice and enjoy intimacy with the Creator. Anyone who reads this book will be blessed."

—GAY LYNN HORN, CODIRECTOR OF YOUTH WITH A MISSION, CIMARRON, CO

"Rarely has anyone written a book with the integrity and intensity of feeling found in *The Luckiest Man*. If you want to learn how to have deep intimacy with God, how to enter into true love with those most precious to you, and how to face your own wrestling with mortality, this is the book for you. Rarely will you read a book written with such insight as this one. You will weep, you will laugh, you will think, you will worship, and you will face yourself as you discover the blessings suffering has brought to John. While none of us wants to suffer, all of us can learn what it means to know God as we never could know him otherwise, an amazing and intimate blessing from the most loving Father we can ever have."

—BILL LAWRENCE, PRESIDENT OF LEADER FORMATION INTERNATIONAL

"My friend John Paine has grown into an extraordinary man of faith. I did not have full appreciation of his strength and life insights until I read *The Luckiest Man*. I was moved to see real examples of the love and grace of our God in the face of John's overwhelming physical and emotional challenges. His story and this book are the real deal!"

—GARY B. WOOD, PhD, FOUNDER OF CONCORDE COMPANIES,
INVESTMENT ADVISOR, PAST CHAIRMAN OF SOCIETY OF
INTERNATIONAL BUSINESS FELLOWS, AND CIVIC VOLUNTEER

"*The Luckiest Man.* What an appropriate title for a man who has taken the best shot the devil has to offer and turned it into the most inspiring, transformational story I have ever read. John Paine shows us without question that no matter our circumstances, we can live a life of joy and peace and purpose. If the Hall of Faith chapter in Hebrews 11 were written today, it would include John Paine. When we have intimacy and a true friendship with God, anything is possible!"

—DON MANNING, ELDER OF VALLEY CREEK CHURCH
AND AUTHOR OF *CRAZY COOL FAMILY*

"Reading *The Luckiest Man* is exactly like meeting John in person—life-changing! In seconds, you feel the peace of God that passes all understanding despite the radical adversity he faces daily with ALS. And then when he starts to share this peace he's found with you, it engulfs you! I am so thankful he's written this to share with others and future generations."

—BOB BEAUDINE, BESTSELLING AUTHOR OF *2 CHAIRS* AND *THE POWER OF WHO!*

"John Paine's testimony and connection to God is one that will touch lives for generations to come! I consider myself 'lucky' that I was able to learn from John's experiences. You will walk away from this book with renewed perspective, a beautiful outlook on life and a desire to share the book with everyone you know."

—KATIE NORRIS, FOUNDER OF *FOTOLANTHROPY*
AND PRODUCER OF *THE LUCKIEST MAN*

THE LUCKIEST MAN

HOW A SEVENTEEN-YEAR BATTLE WITH ALS LED ME TO INTIMACY WITH GOD

JOHN R. PAINE

WITH SETH HAINES

NELSON
BOOKS

An Imprint of Thomas Nelson

Published in Nashville, Tennessee, by Nelson Books, an imprint of Thomas Nelson. Nelson Books and Thomas Nelson are registered trademarks of HarperCollins Christian Publishing, Inc.

Published in association with Yates & Yates, www.yates2.com.

Thomas Nelson titles may be purchased in bulk for educational, business, fundraising, or sales promotional use. For information, please email SpecialMarkets@ThomasNelson.com.

Unless otherwise noted, Scripture quotations are taken from the Holy Bible, New International Version®, NIV®. Copyright © 1973, 1978, 1984, 2011 by Biblica, Inc.® Used by permission of Zondervan. All rights reserved worldwide. www.Zondervan.com. The "NIV" and "New International Version" are trademarks registered in the United States Patent and Trademark Office by Biblica, Inc.®

Scripture quotations marked NKJV are from the New King James Version®. © 1982 by Thomas Nelson. Used by permission. All rights reserved.

Any Internet addresses, phone numbers, or company or product information printed in this book are offered as a resource and are not intended in any way to be or to imply an endorsement by Thomas Nelson, nor does Thomas Nelson vouch for the existence, content, or services of these sites, phone numbers, companies, or products beyond the life of this book.

ISBN 978-1-4002-1002-2 (HC)
ISBN 978-1-4002-1003-9 (eBook)

Library of Congress Cataloging-in-Publication Data

Names: Paine, John R., 1952- author.
Title: The luckiest man : how a seventeen-year battle with ALS led me to intimacy with God / John R. Paine, with Seth Haines.
Description: Nashville : Thomas Nelson, 2018.
Identifiers: LCCN 2018015730 | ISBN 9781400210022
Subjects: LCSH: Amyotrophic lateral sclerosis--Patients--Religious life.|
Paine, John R., 1952- | Spirituality--Christianity.
Classification: LCC BV4910.32 .P35 2018 | DDC 248.8/6196839092 [B] --dc23 LC record available at https://lccn.loc.gov/2018015730

Printed in the United States of America

18 19 20 21 22 LSC 10 9 8 7 6 5 4 3 2 1

To Margaret, my children, and my grandchildren:
you are my every motivation.

The cost to your natural life is not just one or two things, but everything. Jesus said, "If anyone desires to come after Me, let him deny himself. . . ." That is, he must deny his right to himself, and he must realize who Jesus Christ is before he will bring himself to do it. Beware of refusing to go to the funeral of your own independence.

—OSWALD CHAMBERS, *MY UTMOST FOR HIS HIGHEST* (DECEMBER 9)

CONTENTS

CONTENTS

INTRODUCTION

An Invitation

I am inviting you to come with me on a journey, a journey to intimacy with God.

Intimacy with God—the real kind—began in the wee hours of the night after I received my diagnosis as an ALS patient. Consider this peek, this snapshot. On that night, the muscles in my forearm twitched to the rhythm of death, a reminder of how my lifespan had been compressed.

You will die. You will die. You will die.

Accompanying that rhythm was a tornado of feelings I was not ready to experience. What of hope and peace? What of the closeness of God, who is supposed to comfort his children? There was no hope, peace, or comfort, at least not just then. Instead, the room was silent as a tomb.

That's when I did the very thing I'd not yet dared to do. I sat, fully examined all of my emotions, and I lashed out at God. For an hour I felt it all; I spat it all. I might have cursed. I left no word unsaid. I pounded the desk with my fist. And when I thought I'd given God the best piece of mind the created had ever given the Creator, I sat, breathless.

There was silence for a moment. Then, the still small voice of God came.

Are you done yet?

WHEN ALL ELSE FAILS, TELL THE TRUTH.

In the days leading up to my diagnosis, I thought I knew what it meant to live. A successful entrepreneur, I'd bought and sold business after business. I'd reaped the rewards of that success and created a life of comfort and security for my family. A well-regarded churchman, I led packed Bible studies and chaired committees; my tithes and offerings were appreciated by church accountants and finance committees alike. A committed father, I'd reared four children, who were, for the most part, self-sufficient and productive members of society. And though my wife, Margaret, and I had our fair share of marital turmoil, we'd reached a resting place, a place where the choppier waters of marriage seemed to smooth over. I was walking into middle age, and wasn't it all falling into place?

Before death, disease, or tragedy strikes, there are things you think you know. I, for instance, thought I knew almost everything. I knew how to build any building, how to buy and sell businesses, how to change the oil in my car, how to lead a Bible study. And perhaps most embarrassing, I thought I knew what it meant to be intimate with God. I thought knowing all the answers was the same thing as knowing God. I supposed finding favor with my church, with the men in my Bible study, meant finding favor with him. *I thought I knew . . . I thought I knew . . . I thought I knew.*

But what did I know, really?

It's easy to second-guess it all from this wheelchair, but that doesn't make these second-guessings less true. When ALS set in, I lost the use of my fingers, then toes, then arms, then legs, and that's when my illusions of knowing died. Then the pain came, screaming like a banshee, and that put the final nail in the coffin of all that false knowing. What was financial success or accomplishment in light of the pain, in light of total paralysis? What was intimacy with God? Did I really know anything anymore?

The pain—it still haunts; it's the constant reminder of my frailty, the hollowness of all those self-important things of my past, the things I thought brought me so much validation. It's the reminder, too, that though I thought I understood what it meant to know God, I didn't have a clue about what it meant to be intimate with him. This pain, though, is a constant invitation to remember what it means to live in intimacy, that state of connection best described as *oneness*.

Let me explain.

———— ✕ ————

When the pain comes calling—as the pain is wont to do—memories are my medication. I use them like tramadol, like morphine. Memories distract from the pain and remind me of the path I've taken to finding true life. And yes, I have found true life.

Here comes the pain, and I remember how sweet everything seemed before the diagnosis, before the wheelchairs and ventilators. I recall the evening walks through the neighborhood with Margaret, holding her hand. I remember playing catch with my boys or tossing my baby girls high in the air. But so often, I find myself stretching into my favorite set of memories—those many days I spent on the property at Lake Palestine, my sanctuary west of Tyler, Texas.

I first walked the lake property with my father-in-law, who purchased it in 1975. It was a remote property, a quiet place with thousands of feet of shoreline, shoreline I'd later come to own. Over the years, I must have walked that property hundreds of times, and in my memory, I still can. I remember the path from the lake house down to the banks, standing in the rising sun of the morning as the water lapped at my feet. Even now, I can still smell the sweetness of the bluebonnets after a driving spring rain. I can hear the children playing in the woods beside the lake, too, and in this memory, I walk to the sound of their laughter. I see them running the trails, and I join in the chase.

I spent so many days on the banks of that lake with my boys, arm cocked and loaded before flinging a crankbait into the water. There is a tautness in the line after the strike of a fish, and the muscles never forget this. I can sometimes feel the strain in my forearms as I play my memories to shore. I can feel, too, the memory of muscles tightening as I cut the wheel of the ski boat hard to the left, as I swing howling boys over the wake in an effort to shake them from the inner tube. I remember the tremble in my thighs as I squatted over a slalom ski, as I cut through the spray, as I saw the rainbow in that spray, if only for a moment.

So many evenings I walked the perimeter of the property, strolled down the lakefront and through the dense woods at dusk. Even now I can hear the wind rustling through the trees and smell the honeysuckle climbing the bones of a dead pine. I recall the thick, sweet summer air and the symphony of birds rising from the branches overhead. The last rays of light filter through the boughs of my memory, and I remember that on one such evening, God spoke to the quietness of my spirit. I didn't understand his voice in those days, not really. I was too self-sufficient, too absorbed in my own successes and accomplishments. Even still, this was my first inkling of the tangible presence of God.

It's been too many years since I've walked that property. I cannot lose myself in the woods or feel the fight of the bass on a taut line anymore. I cannot hear the squeals of my children or grandchildren on the trails or see the sunlight filtering through the pines. I cannot watch the trail of carpenter ants on the back acreage as they carry pieces of foliage stripped from the trees and bushes, or see the dance of dew and sunlight suspended from the morning's new spiderwebs. I'll never again see the bald eagle, talons stretched to the water before the catch. And though you may be tempted to consider these memories a sort of scourge or plague, they aren't. They are a gift. They serve as the backdrop for the sweetness I've learned to recognize since those days. The truth is, in the days before my diagnosis, I caught only momentary glimpses of life's beauty; today, I've learned to experience the eternal beauty of an intimate connection with family and God.

If I'm honest, before my diagnosis I carried so much noise with me, even on those days I spent at the lake. There, in my personal sanctuary, my mind often stretched to a thousand corners, to the next business venture, the next gala, the next Bible study I'd teach, the next family problem to fix. I filled every spare second, even those quiet lakeside moments, with mental gyrations, hoping to set up another success or to procure another business or property. I might have worked the angles of a dozen deals at any given time, even in the cool of a Lake Palestine evening. I might have visualized the spreadsheets or pro formas sitting on my desk in Dallas. Even when the evening sun danced across the water like a million twinkling stars, when it collected in Margaret's eyes, I was so often somewhere else. I was always on the hustle, always striving, and she knew it full well. If you asked, Margaret might tell you I didn't know how to turn off my drive for success and affirmation. She might have told you I didn't know how to be present or be content. She was right about both.

Margaret may have been the only one who saw through my striving, who knew how all that striving kept me from true intimacy. She knew that though I claimed all the effort in business was to secure a future for her, for my children and grandchildren, it wasn't. She may have known that all the Bible studies I taught, all the money I gave, all the church problems I fixed had little to do with God. So much of it was all for me, for my need for validation. And now, I understand Margaret never asked for the money, the accounts, the properties, the striving, the acts of service—not really. She wanted true intimacy with me, my attention, my mindfulness. She wanted that vulnerable, no-fences kind of marital oneness, a oneness of the heart that's both rare and coveted. And didn't God want those same things?

I cannot walk that property the way I once could, but over the last seventeen years of living with this disease, I've come to understand the gift of intimacy that's produced by God-designed dependence, and it's been life's greatest gift. I have become dependent upon doctors, nurses, and caretakers; upon respirators, lifts, and wheelchairs. I've found myself at the mercy of those around me—my family and friends. And when I was forced to stop and take a long look at the downward trajectory of my life, I realized that my previous notions of self-sufficiency and importance were fabricated from the cloth of my own wounds. Now I know that life is not about being validated by others, or by my accomplishments, or by having hero songs sung about me. Life is about finding our validation in God's unrelenting, uncompromising, unconditional love. This is the lesson I learned only by coming to terms with my own disability and death.

There are a hundred ways to say the same thing. You could say that your past doesn't define you, or that the future isn't something we're promised. You might talk about the bird in the hand or living in the moment. The more spiritual among us might cite the scripture about storing up treasures on earth ("you fool," Luke 12:19–20). But let me say it this way: the only certain gifts granted by God are found in the intimacy of this very moment. These certain gifts are found in intimacy with the people right in front of your nose, in intimacy with God as he speaks love straight to your heart.

When all else fails, tell the truth—I suppose this has been the motto of my life since that fateful day when the doctor handed down her death sentence. And so, consider this truth: every day of my life is spent in physical pain, in paralysis, but even still, my life is full of joy and a sense of fulfillment. These emotions come from this truth of all truths: I know the heart of God toward me; I know what it means to have true intimacy with God. And oh, this intimate love of God—this is the true stuff of life.

This is the story of my metamorphosis, my becoming by unbecoming. It's the story of my slow slide into the meaning of life, my dying to live. And though you may feel tempted to feel sorry for me from time to time, to wallow in the pain of my disease, know this: I don't; you shouldn't either. I'll be honest about that pain—at least as honest as I know how to be—but that pain doesn't negate the fact that I'd not trade any of it if I had to give back the beauty of my present life, the intimate connection with God I've learned to enjoy. I wouldn't trade this intimacy for an eternity of walking with Margaret in the woods near Lake Palestine, or for the opportunity to chase my squealing grandchildren through those woods, to catch them, to hug them one by one.

As you read my story, I want you to know that my fight with the violence of ALS has been my personal pathway to the discovery of intimacy with God. I don't believe it requires suffering to know the full love of God; instead, I think it requires a simple act of unbecoming, of falling into the truth of God's deep desire for you, regardless of your own accomplishments or false successes. If you can find your way into this sort of unbecoming, I bet you'll come to discover the gospel about yourself—you are wholly, unconditionally, and completely loved. Only by this discovery can you experience transformational, intimate oneness with God.

God made you for intimacy. What does that mean? Let's explore it through the story of my metamorphosis, my unbecoming. Join me on a journey to intimacy.

PART I

The Trials

CHAPTER 1

The Luckiest Man

These are the things you cannot comprehend when you are first diagnosed with amyotrophic lateral sclerosis (ALS): in your final days, you will be a functional quadriplegic; if you are one of the less fortunate ones who contracts a rarer, slower-killing, nerve-heightening variant of ALS, pain will be your lot in life; you will be unable to move your arms, legs, or head; a machine will breathe for you; you'll spend the majority of any given day in a chair; in that chair, you'll feel as if one hundred cigarette lighters are burning through your backside, your thighs, your elbows; you will be unmoving, always awake to pain, ever aware of the fragility of your life. The good doctors advise you of these potential ALS symptoms, sure. But how can you understand this kind of disability? It's a thing never understood—not really—even when you're living in those last days. Especially when you're living in those last days.

ALS—also known as Lou Gehrig's disease—is cruel. It robs you of mobility, gives you misery in exchange. It is a disease—perhaps one of many—born from the pit of hell. It comes from its fire. It brings its fire to you. It is your enemy, even if your teacher.

Welcome to my life.

It is the evening before my sixty-third birthday, and tonight we are celebrating. The family has been talking about it for weeks; the children and grandchildren are excited for the red-carpet premiere of the documentary commemorating my life—*The Luckiest Man*. My friends are all abuzz, and some are traveling from across the pond to take part. The theater is sold out; more than eight hundred attendees are expected, they've told me. The local Fox News affiliate is attending. The hosts of a nationally syndicated radio program are coming. It's as much attention as any man could want. It's more than any man needs.

I should be excited. I should be looking forward to it with anticipation. But as happy as I am for this event, it is sure to be a celebration of my pain. I don't know any other way to put it.

How did Fotolanthropy—a group of creative documentarians promoting inspirational stories—manage to make a full-length film of my life after only a few short interviews? I considered the crowds—how would they react to the message? Would anyone come? Then, I considered my pain—how would I make it through a grueling night?

I call Leo, my friend and full-time caretaker, to my bedside and let him know I'm ready to suit up. It's a night for dressing to kill, I tell him, smiling.

He begins at my feet, pulls my custom-made compression socks over my calves so as to slow the inevitable swelling that comes with sitting immobile for hours at a time. He then slides my legs into my suit pants, pulls the pants past my knees, over my thighs, and past my bottom. Leo removes my BiPAP nasal pillow—the mechanical diaphragm that forces oxygen into my lungs. My diaphragmatic capacity has plummeted to less than 10 percent of what it once was, and without this nasal pillow, I'd be a dead man in a matter of minutes. Working against the clock, he centers me in the webbing of a sling laid out on the bed beneath me, which is then attached to an overhead rail lift. He pushes the button, and the limp weight of my body rises above the bed. As I'm lifted, my head slumps forward while the sling pulls my knees closer to my chest. For a moment, I am a child, cradled by a mechanical arm, and in this way Leo carries me across the room. I am still not accustomed to this tenderness.

In this cradled position, even as the pain of pulling joints sets in, I close my eyes and there is Jesus himself, holding me. I can almost feel the strength of his own wounded hands. As I'm carried in the sling, I tell Jesus how much it hurts, how much I want relief. The relief doesn't come, but peace does as I hear the words of my friend.

I will never leave you or forsake you.

I am with you and will comfort you.

The wounded healer knows how to comfort the hurting.

Leo lowers me and places me in the center of my wheelchair's donut-shaped and air-filled seat cushion. Over these last fifteen years, the atrophied muscles of my thighs and bottom have left my hindquarters deflated, and my skin hangs slack. When sitting, my bones press against all this loose skin and rub against the nerves. I feel the pressure and separation of my weakened pelvic bone as it touches the chair's padded seat, then the pulling of my femurs against slack tendons and ligaments. I can feel my skeleton pulling against itself, my hips threatening to displace and my arms attempting to dislocate from the shoulder sockets. The nerves are firing up under my thighs and buttocks, and hot spots light in my backside. These are my familiar enemies. My teachers too.

Leo takes a different BiPAP nasal pillow and inserts the two quarter-inch nozzles that are connected to a rigid plastic tube in each nostril, and

I fall in sync with the whir of the machine. The mask is connected to a portable ventilator that pushes a prescribed amount of pure air into my nose at the proper pressure to fill my lungs. This automated diaphragm pushes, then pauses, then pushes, then pauses again. This mobile, external diaphragm keeps me alive, but only if I fall into its rhythm, only if I breathe when it pushes air and exhale when it pauses.

Inhale.

Exhale.

Breathe in rhythm. Live in rhythm.

This is the secret to staying alive.

Leo unbuttons a starched white shirt and pulls my left arm through the sleeve, then leans me forward. My head slumps toward my knees, my neck no longer able to support the weight of my head. He pulls the shirt around my back, leans me against the chair back, then pulls my right arm through. Leo leans me forward again, this time resting my head between my knees, and he smooths the shirt against my back.

"Do you feel any creases or wrinkles?" he asks.

"None," I say, staring at the floor.

Leo pushes me back against the chair, centers my torso, and makes sure my head is square against the headrest. When centered, gravity doesn't pull me from side to side and there's little threat of my shoulders sliding from the wheelchair back, of the weight of my head slinging me from my chair. It is a task that is easier said than done, but Leo has the caretaker's touch.

He begins working the shirt buttons, then pulls my shirttail down and tucks it around the outside of my pants. My shirts are cropped so that they extend only inches below my belt line. If they extended any farther, the wrinkles would be unbearable.

The shirt fits like a tent. So much for tailor-made. We laugh.

Now twenty-five minutes into the dressing process, Leo reaches under my legs and smooths the fabric to ensure there are no wrinkles. He unzips the fly of my pants, reaches in, lifts each leg, and pulls the loose skin forward. This is standard protocol. Even the smallest wrinkle—whether in the clothing fabrics or in the skin under my legs or arms—sets the nerves ablaze. If large enough, a wrinkle can press against a blood vessel and cut off circulation. Wrinkles once taken for granted are now the instigators of great pain.

I look down at my feet; even with compression stockings, they are already swelling; the blood is beginning to pool. I know that under my stockings, my feet are purple and filling with even more stagnant blood. This swelling is a reminder that without movement, without exercise of the muscles, the heart alone cannot return the blood from the extremities. Beyond a vascular issue, though, this swelling is an impediment to style. I'd love to wear my beautiful leather dress shoes, but the discomfort would be unbearable. I opt for wider, black canvas shoes, and Leo slips them on my feet. They are two sizes too big, and the insole has been removed to afford extra room for my swelling feet—a necessity.

Leo then widens the loop of my purple tie, slips it over my head, tightens the noose under my collar, and turns it down. I feel the silk loop pulling the loose fabric taut, feel the knot pressing against my Adam's apple. I cannot remember the last time I wore a tie. It feels familiar.

Leo checks my position again, and comfortable that I'm centered and all smoothed out, he reaches for my suit coat and repeats the shirt donning process. It has taken us forty minutes. Finally, I am dressed and in the chair.

I've learned to say goodbye to the little things, the everyday things, such as dressing or breathing on my own. Leo picks up the brush, and I try to remember when I said goodbye to straightening my own hair. I can't. He brushes my teeth and takes one last look, making a few last-minute adjustments before holding up a mirror for me. My frame is thin, slight. The fabric of my suit hangs limp. My shirt collar is a little loose. My shoes are functional. My nose is covered with a breathing mask. I hear the whir of my mechanical lungs. I sound like Darth Vader.

I used to judge an unkempt gentleman. Those are not fond memories. Now I've learned not to take appearance past face value. I've learned to see myself the way God sees me—loved, even in this mess of a body.

I love you as you are, the real you, he reminds me, and I know this is true. This ever-present reminder, this sense of intimate nearness—these are true gifts. If only I'd experienced these gifts before my terminal diagnosis.

Leo removes my nasal pillow. Attached to the chair's arm is a joystick, which extends toward my lips. The joystick powers a steering mechanism attached to my wheelchair, and by this I maintain some semblance of mobility. The joystick and the nasal pillow are incompatible, though, so when I am on the move, I am short of oxygen. This life is full of trade-offs.

I set sail, charting a course through my master bedroom and down the hall past the library. I enter the formal living room, cruise past the oversized furniture and the large curio that I purchased for Margaret. The curio holds her collection of antique teapots, which are only special to me because they are of value to her. I've learned to value the things she values. I have little time left to value her.

I stop at the glass wall that looks over the lake behind our home. The sky is growing dark. Yes, heavy rains were predicted, but I didn't expect it to be this black. I turn and enter the kitchen and informal living room. With this new vantage, the western view, the sky is even more ominous.

Storms are little things these days, though. I've come to know the God who speaks through them.

Margaret enters the room wearing a form-fitting gray dress and gold shoes, and the clouds seem to roll away. Diamonds frame her neck. Her hair has thinned from chemotherapy, her own fight against follicular lymphoma, stage four. Even still, she is my radiant bride, more beautiful after all these years. We are quite the pair—Paines in our pain—but just take a peek; we look *good*. We are in the best condition of our lives.

"Ready?" she asks.

I smile. It is my premiere night. I am dressed. I am nervous. It is time.

CHAPTER 2

Deathnosis

It all started with a muscle twitch on the top of my forearm. On a Monday morning just like any other, I sat on a gym bench, curling dumbbells. That's when I noticed it—the quiver.

I curled the dumbbell again; the small muscle group spasmed again. After my workout, I showered and buttoned my starched dress shirt. The tremor fluttered against the fabric. In the car, in the boardroom, on my conference calls throughout the day, the muscle shuddered. It was constant.

I considered it a minor annoyance—just a tweak, a strain, perhaps a function of too many reps with too much weight? I did notice the loss of strength that accompanied the muscle twitch, and that didn't seem to make much sense; hadn't it set in while I was curling, while I wasn't using the muscle groups in my forearm? And if it were a tweak, where was the pain?

Could it be a sign of aging? At forty-seven, I was well past my prime, after all. My body wasn't what it used to be. I decided to give my body a few days to heal. Things would sort out. Hadn't they always?

Tuesday passed, then Wednesday, and the tremor in my forearm continued, sometimes quivering to the point of distraction. During calls, I massaged my arm with my right hand. I squeezed my left hand, balled it into a fist, and pumped it to work blood into the forearm. I rotated my hand, working the muscles. But no matter how much I massaged and tried to loosen the muscles, the top of my forearm shivered against my starched sleeve. Perhaps I just needed to take a break, maybe for just a week or two.

Two weeks passed, and faithful to my morning routine, I returned to the gym, standing under a barbell. I felt fatigued and had loaded the barbell with less weight, hoping to compensate with more repetitions. I pressed the weight up, pushed it toward the ceiling, and though my right arm cleared the weight from the start, my left arm hesitated. There was the shimmy, the twitch, but where was the strength?

While the muscle spasms had been annoying, the loss of strength was concerning. I was a strong man, a competitor. I was capable and accomplished. I was mentally tough. And feeling the misfire in my muscle, I decided to visit my general practitioner. He examined my forearm, asked me to remove my shirt so he could examine my spine. Tracing the bones of my upper back, and with concern in his voice, he suggested I visit a neurologist.

I balked. "A neurologist for a muscle twitch? Maybe I should just lay off the weights for a few days?"

"No," he said. "We might be looking at spinal compression, which can impinge the nerves. If it is, you could lose all feeling in your arm and some of the mobility. A neurological assessment is in order."

Two weeks later, forearm still aflutter, I visited Dr. Maureen Watts, the Dallas neurologist to whom I'd been referred. We discussed my symptoms, and she suggested a round of diagnostics. X-rays were taken.

Additional tests were scheduled. I left the clinic, unalarmed. There were things to do, business ventures to review. I didn't have time to worry.

Another two weeks passed, and I sat again in a hospital gown as a technician wired me up to an electrical current. Adhesive electrodes were placed all over my body, and the technician sent a series of pulses into each muscle group. Every shock produced a contraction or a tingling sensation, and when I asked, she said she was measuring the speed at which the electrical current passed through my muscles and nerves.

After removing the electrodes, the technician turned to a small table where a series of needles that seemed the size of crochet hooks lay. With the delicacy of a medieval torturer, she inserted the needles into my forearms, palms, neck, and every other muscle group she could find. Again, an electronic current was introduced, and I was asked to remain still as a statue. The test produced extreme pain and discomfort as she needled me for what seemed like an eternity.

Another two weeks passed, and Dr. Watts called me back to the office and told me the tests were inconclusive. She recommended referral to a more specialized clinic, a neurological diagnostic clinic at UT Southwestern Medical Center. Even still, I wasn't concerned. It was, after all, just a muscle twitch.

During my first diagnostic visit to UT Southwestern, I met with Dr. Sharon Nations, a specialty neurologist. She informed me that the muscle spasms I was experiencing were called "fasciculations" and indicated she'd want to run her own series of tests.

I was taken to the MRI Imaging Center, where I removed my clothes and donned another white hospital gown, open at the back. A technician inserted a needle into my back and pumped my spinal cavity full of radioactive dye. With my feet strapped to a table, they tipped me upside down so the dye could creep into the upper portion of my spine. There, a magnetic imaging machine photographed my bones as the dye stretched up my skeleton. After the test, I was given no results, but a follow-up for additional testing was scheduled.

Weeks later, and months into the continual fasciculations, I returned to UT Southwestern, where Dr. Nations indicated she'd like to repeat the electro-torture tests completed by my previous neurologist, Dr. Watts.

The tests were run—more needling, more electric currents—but this time, the receptionist did not schedule a follow-up appointment. Days passed without a phone call. It was the middle of September 2000, and with only two weeks before Margaret and I were to take a cruise through the wild waters of Alaska, I called the neuromuscular floor of the hospital.

"I'm traveling with my wife in two weeks, and before I leave, I need an appointment," I said. "And let's be clear. This *will* be diagnosis day."

Diagnosis day came, and when I arrived, the doctors asked me to disrobe again. I was handed the all-too-familiar split-back gown.

"Why do I need this?" I asked.

There were a few more tests, they explained before shutting the door.

A technician came into the room minutes later, a table full of padded electrodes and needles. He said they'd like to repeat what I had come to know as an electromyography test—the test I'd endured twice already— but as he approached, I made myself clear.

"I've done this test twice already. We are not doing it again today. Call my doctor. It's time for some answers."

As I sat on a papered patient table, the updraft from the air conditioner cooled my backside. I'd waited for this day for what seemed like months. The second hand of the white wall clock clicked, and clicked, and clicked. Minutes passed, then a quarter hour, then a half hour. All these months, and what did I have to show for all this waiting, for all these hours in exposed-back hospital gowns? Didn't these doctors realize how busy I was? Didn't they know I had business matters to tend to? Didn't they realize that time is money?

Margaret sat on the chair across from me, her back straight, legs crossed, foot shaking. Her voice was thin as she attempted small talk.

More minutes passed, and I was formulating what verbal jab I might give the doctor, when the door opened. Dr. Nations kept eye contact from the minute she entered the room, expression as flat as the charts she carried. She pulled up a stool, and I smiled in acknowledgment, any witty jab now an afterthought. She stared ahead, still expressionless, and placed a packet of papers on the table across from Margaret. With the look of neither empathy nor dispassion, she turned to me and gave her findings.

"I believe you may have amyotrophic lateral sclerosis."

I said nothing.

"It's known as ALS."

"Plain English, Doctor," I said.

"Mr. Paine, you have Lou Gehrig's disease."

I sat, unblinking, and recalled Lou Gehrig, the star first baseman for the Yankees in the 1920s and 1930s. Some years before, I'd watched *The Pride of the Yankees*, the classic movie about Lou Gehrig's storied career, but the details of the disease that truncated his career weren't coming back to me. It'd taken his life; I knew that much. But wasn't his death horrific? The details escaped me, but I was still unworried. Medicine had come so far in the last seventy years; surely there was a modern treatment.

"What's the plan? How do we beat this thing?" I blustered.

Drier than a Dallas summer, she looked at me and said, "There is no cure. It is a progressive degenerative motor neuron disorder."

I considered each word, looking for the escape hatch. I replayed the sentence, allowed it to tumble over again and again in my brain. I found no traction. My wheels started spinning, slipping.

"What are we talking about here?"

"I'm sorry, Mr. Paine," she said, "but here's the straight answer. You will lose all motor functions over the next few years as the brain cells die, and you will become paralyzed from the top of your head down. Eventually, your diaphragm will stop working. It's a slow process of suffocation."

A metallic ring rose in my ears. My mouth dried.

"What's next? How much time do I have?"

"I suggest you go home and get your affairs in order, Mr. Paine. You have two to five years left."

I looked at Margaret, who sat white-faced in the chair across from me. My life was terminal. Our marriage was terminal. Everything was terminal—the bank accounts, the businesses, the relationships with my children. I would die in two to five years. And then?

The humming in my ears grew.

"I'm so sorry," I said to Margaret. It was all I could muster as tears welled up in my eyes.

There is a faded memory, maybe a recollection. The doctors may have recommended some support groups or handed me a stack of pamphlets. Maybe they told me of next steps, or medications, or providers of the medical equipment I'd need to prolong my life. It's possible Margaret asked questions. Or maybe she didn't. It's hard to remember the aftershocks.

I must have taken off the gap-backed medical gown and put my dress slacks and starched shirt and loafers back on. I must have done these things because I was riding in the passenger seat of the car, the road stretching out in front of us loose as taffy. Margaret drove; it was my first act of relinquishing control.

Outside, the people of the world were walking, holding hands, swinging in swing sets, throwing footballs. Businessmen were hurrying to their next meetings, chasing down the next deal. We entered our neighborhood and saw women chatting on their front steps. A boy biked down the sidewalk. The world was moving as if nothing had changed, all those happy lives just keeping on, but I was in a car, carrying the new weight of a terminal diagnosis, my left forearm trembling all the while.

I followed the broken lines of the road, silent. Margaret didn't speak either. We both looked out the window, surprised by how dark a sunny September day could be. I had spent my whole life trying to make a dent, and now, my life was spent. Now, life was denting me.

We pulled into the garage, and she turned the key. I was struggling to breathe, drowning in disbelief. The muscles in my forearm twitched, fasciculations reminding me in a staccato rhythm.

You will die.

You will die.

You will die.

Time was not on my side. Waste was not an option. That's when the first inklings of anger and denial set in.

"This can't be happening," I said to no one.

Hadn't Margaret and I overcome so much in our lives? Hadn't we made our way through a failing business, a daughter with an eating disorder? Hadn't we come through a near-broken marriage, only to find ourselves good and in love again? Wasn't the last half of my life supposed to be good, maybe even the best? I was only forty-seven, and the prognosis was worse than grim.

"Get your affairs in order," she had said.

Thanks, Doctor. Thanks, God.

Two to five years. That was the diagnosis. And then, I would stop breathing. To death.

CHAPTER 3

The Cloud of Witnesses

Margaret comments on my tie, smiles, and flashes her eyes. It's been more than thirty years since we were in high school, but she still manages that schoolgirl look of love. She turns and walks out of the room, telling me she'll meet me at the van. Hillary, our youngest daughter—now an adult—wants to ride with us, she says.

While I was looking out the window, Leo must have placed the nasal pillow back into place, though I don't remember it. His work is so discreet sometimes. He is beside me, and he checks my position in the chair one last time. Satisfied, he raises the chair's arm back to the center of my chest and places the joystick in front of my lips.

"Let's go," I say, as I push the joystick forward slowly, and my wheelchair obeys. From the kitchen, we make our way to the side of the van—a tricked-out Honda VMI Northstar, converted to carry me in my wheelchair. Using the joystick, I navigate the van's ramp to the center of the vehicle, where a locking mechanism clamps my wheelchair into place.

Pulling away from the house, we drive through the same city streets that taunted me on the day of my diagnosis fifteen years ago. I remember the anger, the vitriol at a God who'd allowed such a drastic change to my life. I've left that anger behind, and maybe that's because being healthy never exempted me from adversity in the first place. Doesn't everyone struggle, the sick and well alike? And if a season is happy and healthy for my neighbor or for the businessman across town, even if they are free from adversity, I can say this now with full release—God bless their happy lives. Seasons like that are a gift.

Walking is a gift.

Hugging your wife is a gift.

Feeding yourself is a gift.

Oh, how I've learned to recognize gifts.

Leaving the neighborhood, we turn toward the theater. On the highway, the rain falls in heavy Texas sheets. I wonder whether anyone will make the event. Even if I were healthy, would I brave this weather, this gridlock, to see a movie about a dying man? Wouldn't I have better things to do? I know this for certain: Fifteen years ago, I wouldn't have felt the need to go to my own premiere. I would have been too busy to listen to my own life. But everything is slower now. The important things are more important. This perspective has been both the gift and curse of ALS—I've learned to identify the truth of living, but I also remember all the unimportant things I've chased.

Use tonight for someone else, I pray. It is a short and simple prayer. I smile as I consider the God who uses small things—the gray slog, adversity, maybe even the story of a dying man—to change the perspective of his people. I consider the God who reminds us that he is found in the simplest routines, even the routines of my own simple life.

Wake.

Pray.

Eat.

Breathe, breathe, breathe.

Love without condition.

Be loved.

Repeat.

We pull past the front of the theater and enter the parking garage, where a space is reserved for the van. Leo exits, walks to the side, and opens the door. We reverse the loading process, and in a few short minutes, my chair is on the ground and the joystick is in my mouth. Margaret and Hillary stand waiting for me. When I'm ready, we make our way to the first floor, where we head toward the entrance. Outside, I see the movie posters in shadow boxes attached to the columns. I pass the posters of Nicole Kidman and Julia Roberts. Bradley Cooper stares from the poster of his new movie. There is a poster across from him, and the face staring from behind the glass of that shadow box is laughing. It's a more familiar face. Mine. I don't have any Academy Awards, and my classic good looks and firm body have gone the way of this devil's disease. Even still, I wonder if the posterized Cooper is a little jealous in his recognition of the truth—I really am the luckiest man.

Two years earlier, Katie Norris, the CEO of Fotolanthropy, heard my story through my pastor. She was looking for inspirational stories, she said, stories of those who have beaten the odds. My pastor gave her my name, and she called, said she'd like to make a documentary of my life. I informed her I wasn't all that inspirational. I was just a dying man, and I'd pass on the offer, thanks.

A year and a half passed, and Katie couldn't shake my story. She met with my eldest daughter, Amanda, and convinced her I needed to be the subject of Fotolanthropy's next documentary. Amanda came to me, painted a picture of how my story could impact others, and that was all the persuasion I needed. Now, here I am, staring at the poster in the gold frame, the title *The Luckiest Man* floating above my head.

I make my way into the lobby, where people are already congregating. Before I can greet them, a photographer wheels me to the left, where a red carpet waits. At the end of the red carpet, my family stands in front of a premiere backdrop with the title of the film splashed across it. Reminders are everywhere. Could I be any luckier? We smile together—the family Paine—as the photographer captures the moment.

The producers of the film tell me it's time to go to the greenroom, and I follow, smiling to the crowd as best as I can with a one-inch piece of plastic crammed up my nose. Steering a wheelchair through a crowd via lip-controlled remote control is no easy task, but I push through the crowd and motor in the proper direction.

The greenroom is a theater stocked with catered food and drinks. The filmmakers tell me I can relax here, as if relaxing is a thing afforded to ALS patients. Crowds, meet-and-greets, even large dinner parties—these are the kinds of things that suck my energy dry these days. And though we've closed the greenroom to all but close friends, family, and those who are in the documentary, there are still more than a few people here. Even still, these are my people. They are very important to me. They take my mind off the pain.

Bart Hansen, a courageous-hearted minister and a friend from California, approaches and leans down to greet me. He's made the journey all this way.

A. C. Musgrave, my former business partner, stops by to talk. Could there be a more faithful friend?

Next in line, Gary and Sheryl Wood come laughing. They have been loyal, never treating me as crippled or different, even as I lost my motor functions.

The crowd begins to press in until it is near-suffocating, and as I look at all the faces, all the people who've come to be a part of my special night, I am struck by the realization that I will not have time to speak with everyone. These smiling people, my people—not all of them will get a piece of me tonight.

I see Robbie, my childhood friend from Tyler. He's flown in from his mission base in Italy just to be a part of this event. I tell him he shouldn't have, as good Texans are prone to say. He laughs, says he wouldn't have missed it for the world, as good Texans are prone to respond. Robbie traveled halfway across the world just to celebrate my life. How could I be more humbled?

Thank you, God, for persistent friends.

Thank you, God, for present friends.

I look at Robbie, smiling. "Who knew two boys from Tyler could be used so much?" I ask, pausing every few words to imbibe oxygen from my nasal pillow.

Robbie laughs. "Who knew?"

More than fifty years of water have passed under the bridge of our friendship. I think back to our early days in Tyler. Hadn't he always been a missionary? Hadn't he always been the kind of guy who carried good news with him wherever he went?

I consider our childhood. Mine was all uphill and dyslexic and struggle, and Robbie was my friend through it all. The memory brings a flood of emotion, recollection of my brother, my parents. My mother and father were just a couple from Texas who did the best they knew how. Sometimes childhood was dark, sometimes beautiful. But my folks—they loved me. I miss them. I wish they could be here to see this, the night I am being crowned the luckiest man. Maybe they're peeking through heaven's veil, even now. Maybe my older brother is too. If they are, I know they're proud.

CHAPTER 4

Wounded

I was born under the star of Texas, the son of a Texas toolman and a school cafeteria lunch lady. We were a working-class family of low means, a make-do sort of people. Our standard fare was pot roast or tough cuts of chicken-fried steak, always paired with day-old bread slathered with ketchup. On special occasions, mother broke out the Neapolitan Mellorine for dessert, an ice cream alternative rendered from animal lard and vegetable fats. We were neither elegant nor refined. We could not have found high society with a stepladder. The Paines of Tyler were a family made from Texas dust and bootstrap leather.

I was a rough-hewn boy with thick thighs, a protruding hind end, and narrower shoulders. I inherited my older brother, Walker's, hand-me-downs, and they never seemed to fit. My academic constitution was not strong; I had great difficulty reading, and I couldn't seem to put the letters together in an order that quite made sense. In classroom spelling bees, I was always the first out. In the fifth grade, the teachers discovered that I couldn't see the blackboard from my desk, and after a series of eye exams, I was issued a pair of thick, black-rimmed glasses, which were not stylish in 1963. And if all this weren't enough, I wet the bed well into elementary school.

During our childhood years, I suppose we all receive messages, and these were the messages I received most: Walker was exceptional. I was slow. I was ugly. I was a baby. And these messages were not implicit. I did not fabricate them from the raw materials of my young life experience. These messages were explicit, sent by the man I loved the most—my father.

Dad was tougher than tire rubber, and he seemed to believe that the deficiencies of others could only be cast out by way of humiliation. He did not know tenderness and was quick with a harsh word and slow with a hug. He was fond of reminding me how slow I was, as if by some miracle of madness he might goad me into becoming more competent in the classroom. But his criticism wasn't relegated to slights about my intellect. He poked fun at my body shape, noting that my rear was wide and my shoulders were narrow. He took to calling me "Coke bottle" on account of my disproportioned physique, and when he was in a particular mood, he'd call me "two butts" or "twin butts," joking that either half of my gluteus maximus was larger than the entirety of any normal person's hind end. He teased me about my glasses, told me that if I exercised my eyes more I wouldn't need the thick clunkers. And it was with particular delight that my father shared these deficiencies with whoever would listen.

Even if those insults had been tolerable, others were not. On occasion, when Walker and I brought friends home from the football field for a glass of lemonade, my father would meet us in the kitchen and ask whether the baby wet the bed the night before. He'd wait for my answer before cutting the awkward silence. "Some babies just don't grow out of diapers," he'd say.

It's hard to reconcile my father's caustic banter with my enduring love for him, but as I grow older, I see behind his behavior. He was the fifth child in a family of six, and his three oldest siblings were boys. His father—my grandpa—was sick for most of my father's life and passed away when Dad was twelve. So, the older brothers fulfilled the paternal role of the family, young as they were. They ribbed and antagonized him—as teenage boys tend to do—and this became the pattern for my own father's parenting. My father mimicked what he'd been taught, dysfunctional though it was. I guess he was doing the best he knew how, but wounds beget wounds. This is the way of life.

If my father was a tough man, my mother was his exact opposite. Mother loved in a more classic, June Cleaver sort of way. She encouraged us. She talked about spiritual things with Walker and me and sometimes prayed for us. She made us lemonade, cookies, and chocolate pie and did the things good mothers did in the 1950s and 1960s. I felt safe and loved with my mother. She wanted nothing more than to serve others, whether her family, friends, or strangers high-centered in the hospital.

Mother did not insult me to my face, though on occasion I overheard her telling a friend I was slow when she thought I was out of earshot. Still, she did her best to help me overcome what I now know was a learning disability.

During the school year, Walker and I walked home from school together. There, Walker dropped off his books and assignments, which he'd already completed at school, and went out to play or spend time with his friends. I, on the other hand, was slower to finish my work on account of my reading deficiencies, and instead of heading out to the sandlot, I sat at the table with Mother, who labored with me through my homework. While Walker and my friends ran sandlot games of football, Mother and I ran reading drills. While my friends played pitch and catch, Mom pitched words my way, hoping that it would be the magical day when the lights would turn on. But as grateful as I was for her time, as I wrestled down my schoolwork at that kitchen table, one thought kept needling in the back of my mind—*why didn't anyone else have to work this hard to learn to read? Why was I so different?*

I internalized the messages of the world around me—John Paine is slow, ugly, a baby. I internalized, and internalized, and internalized. As those feelings of inadequacy, stupidity, and shame set in, I turned inward. Feelings, after all, were not something Paine men shared, or so my dad said. Feelings proved dangerous, and in the event tears were involved, there followed a spewing of names—imbecile, juvenile, baby, baby, baby. And so, I created a shell, a wall against the world, and I hid behind that wall. I buried my feelings under the wall so as to remove them from the equation. I would not give my father another reason to pick on me. I might be the slow one, but I'd not compound the problem by being the emotional one or the needy one. I'd not let him see me cry or react at all. I'd not show any more weakness than I already carried.

I hid behind the wall of my own creation, and I worked to create a different self-image, a competent, self-sufficient persona I could project on the other side of the wall. Image, image, image—so much of our lives is about projecting a false self-image, isn't it? It would take years to construct that false image of self-sufficiency and perfection, but it would evaporate in a few short hours on the day of my diagnosis. Today, there is nothing left of that false image. This wheelchair is proof of that.

———✕———

Looking back on my childhood, I can say it now—I was verbally abused. I didn't have words for it at the time. After all, these were the days before the proliferation of pop psychology, the days before family therapy was in fashion. I wasn't aware that my father's verbal jousts, the messages he sent, were creating such deep wounds, and even if I had been, I wasn't equipped with the tools to confront him.

My father was a hard worker, and he worked long hours as a traveling salesman for Snap-on Tools, that is, until just after my twelfth birthday. On a day like any other, Walker and I walked in the back door from school. Dad was there, standing in the kitchen, and he was crying—an unthinkable thing in those days. He was leaning into my mother, and he seemed broken somehow, tender. This was not the man I knew.

At supper that night, my father broke the news. His territory at Snap-on had been cut in half because the company had decided to bring in a second tool salesman. The one-half reduction of his territory meant a one-half reduction in his income, and this did not bode well for the family's economic outlook. Things had to change, he said. And change they did.

Over the following week, my father sat at the kitchen table, scribbling out a business plan. By the following Monday morning, he was ready, and he hugged Mother, climbed in his car, and drove to Dallas to begin calling on other tool manufacturers. He called on several tool companies—S-K Wayne, Proto, and a few others—and pitched his services as a tool distributor. Each company contracted with him on the spot, and by the time he returned to Tyler that evening, a new company was born—Bob Paine Tool Company. That same evening, Dad drove to the Snap-on offices and tendered his resignation.

You can't trust anyone but yourself and your family. The world is rigged for adversity, and the only person capable of overcoming it is you. Trust only yourself and your family. Be independent, self-sufficient. These are the lessons he taught us, and he taught them in a thousand different ways. He taught us by starting his own business, sure. But he'd also tell us these things over supper or while working in the yard. Though I might fault him for his verbal abuse, for the way he tore at me day after day, now I can see he thought he was toughening me up; he thought he was preparing me for a world that takes advantage of every tender and slow child. Dad thought he was doing me a favor. It's hard to fault a man for that.

I see through so many of the things my father believed, and in my older age I know them to be false. The measure of men is not found in their toughness, their independence and self-reliance, though so many believe this is true. Self-reliance is a fool's gamble, and there's no such thing as independence—not really. If ALS has taught me anything, it's the beauty of proper dependence on God and others. But if ALS has taught me anything else, it's perspective. And with new eyes, I can look back and see it—Dad wanted the best for us, even if he didn't know how to say it.

⸺✕⸺

Leo stands above me, holding a handkerchief. Thinking about my parents, I've misted up around the eyes, and Leo dabs at the corners. He is my right hand. My left one too.

Before I can thank him, Leo pulls out another handkerchief and wipes my nose. This drainage is a by-product of ALS too—one that's more than a little annoying. And as runny as my nose is, my mouth is always dry on account of the constant draft of air being pushed through it on the way to my lungs. I ask Leo for a drink, and he holds up a cup, straw to my lips. I slump my head forward as slow as I can manage and tuck my chin in to close off my windpipe so as not to choke. I take three gulps, swallowing enough to fill a ten-gallon hat.

Yes, that hits the spot.

Leo takes the cup and wipes my nose again. Perhaps I've become a big baby again, dependent as I am on others. I'm fine with that now.

"Is everything still centered and smooth?" he asks.

"Yes," I say, which is not to say I'm pain-free. He asks if I need to recline.

"Not yet," I say. "We have a long night ahead of us."

Leo knows me as well as any human. He is an extension of me. We are together in this, and I'm grateful. I'd trust him with my life. In fact, I do.

CHAPTER 5

More Than Xs and Os

M y son Josh, who's standing watch at the greenroom door, enters my circle of friends. "It's time to go to the reception area," he says, then adds, "You wouldn't believe how many people are out there, Dad."

Margaret looks at me and smiles as surprise creeps into my brow. "See, Bubby," she says, "I told you people would come." If I could shrug my shoulders, I would. She stoops down to kiss me, just as she does before every meal. She is my favorite girl and always has been.

"Are you ready?"

She knows I'm hurting; I can see it in her eyes. A cascade of fire runs from my hips to my thighs. My hands are freezing, and my feet are ice blocks stuffed into my canvas shoes. The remedy for the pain is to concentrate on the present, on the people, on Margaret, so I look into her deep brown eyes. I could fall into those dark pools even after all these years. I follow the curve of her lips out to the red edges. She is beautiful, a painkiller.

I nod, tell her I'm ready to go, and Leo removes my nose pillow and raises the mechanical arm with the joystick to my lips. My breath draws up short as my mechanical diaphragm stops pushing oxygen into my lungs. I'll never get used to this trade-off—oxygen for mobility—but I push it from my mind and consider the crowd I see through the opening greenroom door. Taking the joystick into my mouth, I push toward this mass of people.

In the hall leading to the lobby, I see the people smiling their hellos. The crowd is thicker than I'd imagined, lining both sides of a roped-off runway through the crowd. Why have these people given up their nights to be here, to celebrate my story? I suppose this is one of life's rare moments, a moment I might have once wanted, only under different circumstances. Once, I would have loved this crowd gathering in celebration of my accomplishments. Once, I would have taken this as a moment of affirmation; I'd have internalized this moment as one of self-importance. Tonight, I don't relish the attention.

Father, use tonight; use this documentary. This is my constant silent prayer.

I hear Margaret behind me, talking, and I think of how lucky I am to have her. She's always been my cheerleader, my encourager, my support. She believed in me before I believed in myself. She is a gift.

In sophomore biology at Robert E. Lee High School in Tyler, a tall, long-legged girl in a miniskirt pranced into the classroom. It was the 1960s, the decade of the miniskirt, and she was handcrafted to model the fashion of the day. I watched her pause in the doorway and survey the room, looking for a desk. She chose her place, then sashayed to it knowing every eye was on her. She was a girl who knew how to enter a room, I thought; she'd been trained in the art of confidence.

I was smitten.

Margaret became my first high school date; she was only fifteen. We went to the inaugural school dance of the year—a Western sock hop—and it only took that night to realize that she was my dream girl. I would do whatever it took to continue seeing her. And so, after my brother and his date drove us to her home after the dance, I followed her to her front door and leaned in for my first taste of those ruby lips. That kiss sealed the deal, though I assure you it was not because of any natural ability on my part. We've been inseparable ever since.

I knew it from the beginning—I really liked this girl. We flirted at school, spent evenings together at her home, and entertained the same friendship circles. She asked me to attend worship services at the Fifth Street Presbyterian Church, and I agreed.

The Hill family lived a confident faith, which was new to me. I was comfortable in church on account of my mother's faithfulness in dragging me to the Sunday services at St. Paul's Methodist Church. (My father was not a religious man.) What's more, I'd prayed with my friend Robbie to accept Jesus when I was fourteen and had even read a few proverbs, hoping some of Solomon's smarts might rub off on me. Faith, though, did not occupy a central role in my life. I didn't even own a Bible. Though I knew families that attended church together, I'd never experienced the kind of earnest family devotion the Hills embodied. They talked about spiritual things together, prayed together, and were mainstays in their church. They spoke of a loving God, a God who cared about them. Their faith touched on every aspect of family life, and as if to draw me into that family faith further, Margaret presented me with a Bible—a black, red-letter King James Version—during our first Christmas together. She was sending the not-so-subtle message—any man who dated her would need to walk in the faith of her father, Don Hill.

I suspect Mr. Hill understood my family situation better than I did, and from the beginning, he took me in as one of his own. During the autumn of 1969, Mr. Hill became a religious attender of every Robert E. Lee High School football game. Of course, he came to watch Margaret perform with the drill team at halftime, at least that's what he said. But I suspect he came to watch his surrogate son run the football through opposing linebackers, because I had no bigger fan in the stands than Mr. Hill. He cheered me on, rooted for me the way any proud father would for his son, and after every game, he was quick with encouragement.

I was the fullback in a wishbone offense—a run heavy scheme of the 1960s—which meant I learned to take a beating on every play. And despite my lack of confidence in every other area of life, I was a different John Paine on the football field. I couldn't see worth a squint in a storm, but I didn't let that stop me. With a strong lower body and a drive to prove myself to my father, I'd take the ball, pick out the blurred color of the opposing linebacker, and run straight through him. My tenacity earned me the nicknames "Paine the Train" and "Big John." What's more, it earned me a scholarship.

The summer after my senior year arrived, and after three years of dating Margaret, the time came for me to make my way to Brownwood, Texas, home of Howard Payne University, where I'd run the pigskin. Margaret had no desire to follow me to the West Texas dust den that hid a rattlesnake under every rock. She'd wait for me, she said, and I knew she would.

The miles—280 of them to be exact—were difficult. We mailed letters to each other every other day. I visited Margaret whenever I could, but still, it was not enough. Just before Christmas break, she drove to

Brownwood. On the first night, we drove the streets of Brownwood, and she cried in the passenger seat. She was miserable without me, she said, and the truth was, I was just as miserable without her.

"I'll follow you anywhere," she said, "but I don't think I can follow you to Brownwood." I tried my best to console her, but it wasn't consolation she wanted. Instead, she wanted clarity.

"What are you going to do with your life?" she asked.

I sat for a moment, flummoxed. I hadn't thought much about it—not really—but I knew that answer would not earn me any points. And so, I gave her the best answer I could.

"I guess I'll be a football coach."

This was not the answer she was looking for; I could tell by her sagging expression. She looked down, put her hands on her knees, took a breath, and said, "Do you think we can live on a coach's salary?"

We.

I considered her challenge, rolled it around a time or two before responding. It was clear—she was considering all the angles. She was miles down the road of our collective life. I'm not sure I was even on the road. I'm not sure I had a map to the road. I was directionless, and in that moment, I knew it.

I did not believe I was capable of being anything more than a struggling C student.

I did not believe I was capable of reading anything more rigorous than the *X*s and *O*s on a locker-room chalkboard.

I did not believe.

I sat in my own shortcomings and puzzled together how I might provide for Margaret, how I might create some semblance of the life she'd always had. She'd grown up well-to-do by Tyler standards. Mr. Hill was the owner of a strong local business and was well respected within the community. Her home was well-appointed, even if it was modest. Her parents were members of the Tyler Petroleum Club. Mr. Hill always had cash on hand. Margaret was not spoiled, but she never wanted for anything. By watching the Hills, I saw a whole different way of living. And I liked it.

Could I give Margaret this kind of lifestyle? Would I risk more failure to find out?

I set my jaw and charted a new course. "I think I'd like to be a general contractor, like your father," I said.

Margaret considered it, nodded. Without any hesitation, and with the assertive spunk I'd so fallen for, she said, "Come home next weekend. Dad is the perfect person to talk to, and I'll make sure he is ready for you."

I returned to Tyler the first week of Christmas break, sucked up my pride, and walked into the Hill home almost unable to contain my excitement. By the time I walked out, Mr. Hill and I had formulated a plan. I'd drop out of Howard Payne and join Mr. Hill's construction crew. I'd save up for the following school year, and I'd enroll in Texas A&M's construction management program. It was a rigorous program, Mr. Hill said, but it'd prepare me for most anything in the industry. And though I didn't know if I could survive the A&M academics, I knew I had to try. Margaret was worth it.

———✕———

After all these years of surrender, life is clearer. The people in this theater have gathered to celebrate me. They've collected in this space, for this time, to hear the story of my life and to learn the lessons of my disease. Before I contracted ALS, before I was confined to this hell of a wheelchair, I would have believed that I deserved this kind of attention. Who couldn't learn a thing or two from me, a self-made man?

Self-made—what a sick half-truth.

Success does funny things to your psyche. It blinds you to the truth behind the truth. But maybe it's easier to remember the truth when you're blessed with a terminal diagnosis. Maybe it's easier to remember the truth in the presence of these many witnesses. Maybe it's nostalgia coloring everything the shade of Margaret's lipstick. Whatever the case, living in the present, I see it with greater clarity. It was Margaret who saw the things in me I couldn't see in myself. It was Margaret who knew how to turn my need for approval and validation into something positive. It was Margaret who knew I was capable of more than a football field could ever offer. It was Margaret who expanded my gift of faith. It was Margaret who taught me the importance of Scripture.

It was Margaret.

It was Margaret.

All along, it was Margaret.

What was Margaret, though? She was the conduit for God's grace, the one who taught me to see myself the way God sees me. God got to me through her. She was a grace.

If you had asked me years before my diagnosis why Margaret caught my attention, I would have laughed and said it was the miniskirt. If you had pushed harder, I'd have told you it was her spunk and spark, her grit that hooked me. But after sixty-three years of living and fifteen years of learning to die, I know what had drawn me to Margaret Hill. It was the way she loved me past my own reservation, past my own fears. She loved me even though I didn't love myself. She loved me enough to give me a vision for what could be. She loved me the way God loves me, and for too long, I took that for granted.

CHAPTER 6

Who's Stupid?

I make my way down the hall, and I'm struck by the sheer volume of people in attendance. This crowd is thick. Who am I to attract this kind of attention, especially in these years of my failing health?

I navigate as best I can, but the going is slow, and I can feel my breath growing short. I'm running out of air. I stop, spit the joystick from my mouth, and begin to turn toward Leo, hoping to get his attention, but before I can, he is there. Having already anticipated the need, he loops the straps of the ventilator over my head and inserts the nozzles of the nasal pillow in my nose.

Josh is behind me, and I feel the strength in his hands as he squeezes my shoulder. That grip—it is so strong. Without the joystick I'm immobile, and as strong as Josh may be at 350 pounds, my chair is too heavy to push through this crowd. Josh removes the attendant joystick velcroed to the back of my chair—a video game-like joystick that's tethered to the back of my chair with three and a half feet of cable—and navigates me through the crowd of people. He could ask Leo to steer, I suppose—it's what Leo is paid to do, after all—but the best sons are glad to serve their old men. Josh is one of the best sons.

I consider the days of Josh's rebellion, those teenage years, when he was doing *who knows what with who knows whom.* He's always been like me, I suppose—hardheaded and strong-willed. But like my relationship with Margaret, our relationship didn't change until I changed; our relationship didn't thaw until God thawed my heart. We've grown as close as any father and son could. Now, here we are, connected by more than this tethered joystick; we are connected in intimate relationship. True intimacy—isn't it found in the tethered connection, in proper dependence upon and trust in each other? This is the way it is with God, too, isn't it? It's taken me so long to learn this lesson.

My eldest son, John, walks in front of me, shaking hands with the folks he knows, smiling at those he doesn't. He's natural with a crowd, genuine. He's one of the kindest men I know. I watch as he welcomes the people, and I'm struck by how many strangers have come. I notice many friends, a few old acquaintances from Dallas, Tyler, and around the country, and then I notice more—business associates, church friends, my old lawyer. Still, a third of these people are strangers. Only the good Lord and their significant others know why they've come.

As I consider the faces in this crowd, the old need for approval and validation comes knocking, if only for a second. I hear the voices of the old demons—

What if they don't like the film?

What if your story is not compelling enough?

What if you're not enough for them?

What if you cause them to waste a night of their lives, a night they can never get back?

I've had years of practice with this sort of taunting, though. I recognize the voices born from old wounds, and I've learned to hush those voices, to recognize their lies. I've long since learned that my value, my identity, has little to do with whether or not others approve of me, my story, my talents, or my accomplishments. Can any man give us eternal validation? No. It's taken me all these years, all this sickness, but I've come to learn that I can only find validation by falling into the unconditional love and acceptance of God. Intimacy means falling into a rhythm of dependence, every day falling into his unconditional love and acceptance. It produces the deepest level of connection that satisfies the heart beyond words.

I sink into the rhythmic whir of the ventilator, into breathing, and into the sense that I am filled by the person and purpose of God. I sink into his rhythm, into the rhythm of any potential outcome, openhearted and willing. Perhaps this crowd will find some meaning in this film; perhaps they won't. Either way, God is here, and he values me just as I am—wheelchair, ventilator, and all.

Here we go, Lord, I pray.

At the end of the hall, we make a right turn into an open lobby. There, the majority of the eight hundred attendees have gathered, and as I enter, they clap as if I'm an A-list celebrity. I look up at Josh. He is the Brad Pitt to my George Clooney.

"I guess a few people did show up," I say, smiling.

He nods.

The lobby is lined with movie posters of some of the greats—Charlie Chaplin, Cary Grant, John Wayne. I reckon these are the ones worthy of applause. Still, I can't help but chuckle.

Move over, Charlie, I think. *This is my night.*

"Move over, John," Charlie might respond. "This is God's night."

I smile. Life is too short to bypass imaginary conversations with the greats.

At the far end of the lobby, Josh navigates me up a wheelchair ramp and onto a stage, where he turns me to face the crowd. All eyes are on me, and I can neither stand to speak, nor wave, nor nod my head in acknowledgment. I can smile, though, so as I lock eyes with many dear friends, I acknowledge them with the broadest smile I can muster. I hope they sense how much I appreciate their presence.

As I take the time to focus on the faces in the crowd, I recognize friends I haven't seen for years, each disguised in his or her Sunday best, faces masked with age. I try to stay attuned to the rhythm of the ventilator. My, how awkward this is.

There's a podium in the center of the stage, and my oldest daughter, Amanda, steps behind it. She warms up the crowd, tells them how honored our family is that they would attend the showing. She explains that there are not many days of victory or celebration for ALS patients or their loved ones, but tonight she promises there will be hope. Her remarks are brief, and she concludes with this: "Over these last fifteen years, we've seen God's hand at work in our family's life. And this movie, it's a reflection of God's ability to take pain and struggle and destruction and hardship and turn it into something beautiful."

The pain—the death of businesses, the family addiction and recovery, the years of cold marriage—if only she knew the depths of my pain. My pain runs deeper than this disease. That's the way of this life.

Amanda thanks the crowd once again and steps behind me.

Jason Castro, a singer-songwriter of *American Idol* fame, takes the stage, and guitar in hand, he plays the Leonard Cohen classic, "Hallelujah." His voice is young and pure; it is bereft of the pain of too many years of living.

He sings the closing hallelujahs and sweeps into a more familiar chorus:

Then sings my soul, my Savior God, to Thee,
How great Thou art; how great Thou art!

These songs hold the secret to life, I think. For so many, it all goes wrong, doesn't it? It did for me. But after it all went wrong, I learned to sing whatever broken hallelujah I had left. I learned the truth behind the words, "How great Thou art!" Maybe that's what tonight is—one last shot to sing the medleys of broken hallelujahs and salvation songs.

Thank you, Lord, I pray. *How great thou art.*

Before it all went wrong, Margaret and I were young and so full of hope. We were beautiful in our naïveté.

I didn't return to Howard Payne University for the spring semester of 1972. Instead, I stayed in Tyler, lived at home, and worked on Mr. Hill's construction crew. I scrimped and saved every penny for tuition at Texas A&M. I took night classes at Tyler Junior College and carved out as much time for Margaret as I could afford without failing my classes. I continued to struggle academically, and these struggles made me question whether I could make the cut in the more rigorous architecture and engineering program at Texas A&M. I was determined to take one challenge at a time, though, and the first challenge was to learn as much as I could about the construction trade.

The men on the construction crew were good men, hardworking and blue-collar. They showed me the ropes, taught me how to hang a door like a bona fide carpenter. But as valuable as they might have been in teaching me the craft of carpentry, their encouragement to continue my education was, perhaps, more valuable. Over water breaks or during lunch, they'd tell me they'd made the decision to bypass long-term education when they were my age; they grabbed their hammers right out of high school and had regretted it ever since. Watching men such as Mr. Hill, they'd learned that there was a lot more to life than getting up and working hard every day just to make ends meet. If I wanted to provide for Margaret, they said, I'd need to do whatever it took to succeed, including pursuing a college degree.

The message was clear. I'd need to learn every trick of the trade these men knew and then some. I'd need to learn the advanced stuff taught in the construction, architecture, and engineering classrooms. And though I was plagued by self-doubt, by questions about whether I could make it into the program at Texas A&M, much less pass any of the courses, I was committed to proving to myself and Margaret that I could succeed, that I could provide.

In the spring of 1972, before I left for A&M, I dedicated myself to the craft of construction. My hard work and ability to deliver quality workmanship was recognized, and while hanging doors in a new commercial building, I overheard C. B. Roberts—the job superintendent on the project I was working—speaking with Mr. Hill. "We really have a sharp one in that Paine kid," he said. "He does every job right the first time, then runs to the next job without being asked. In fact, some of the other carpenters are thinking about talking to him; they think he's making them look bad."

I don't suppose Mr. Roberts intended me to hear those remarks, but they were a shot of confidence, an ego boost from a man I respected so much. In such a fragile time in my life, that compliment from Mr. Roberts was one of the footings on which I'd build a career.

The spring semester gave way to summer, and by May 1972, I'd worked hard to prove myself an asset to Mr. Hill's crew. My wages were meager, but each week I saved nearly every penny for investment in my future with Margaret. What money didn't go to pay for night classes at Tyler Junior College, I saved for my coming tuition needs at Texas A&M. The weeks turned to months, and in no time, the spring semester of 1973 was upon us. Margaret and I enrolled in Texas A&M and set out for College Station, Texas. I was excited for the upcoming semester, but fearful and intimidated as I was by any academic pursuit, I didn't review the course catalog. Instead, I focused only on the classes for the semester.

It was weeks into that first semester, and I was struggling to keep up with the reading assignments. A classmate surmised my difficulty and introduced me to a new concept—speed-reading. Instead of reading a word at a time, he said, I should consider taking in larger chunks. The concept, at least as he explained it, was to survey entire paragraphs, to take them as a sort of word picture. I was skeptical, but since I'd always struggled with reading, I figured I had little to lose. I started by surveying sentences, and with only a few weeks of practice, I could take in paragraph-sized portions of text. I found that this sort of reading was similar to the multidimensional way I'd learned to read schematics and blueprints on the job site, and when I closed my eyes after looking at a paragraph, I could almost envision the meaning.

I can't quite explain why, but the practice of speed-reading and multi-dimensional thinking was a sort of key that began to unlock my academic potential. I began reading faster than I ever had, and my reading comprehension levels skyrocketed. If this were not enough, I was surprised to find that when I stepped away from my textbooks, even for long periods of time, I could still see the words. They danced in my imagination and connected ideas and concepts. In less than a semester, school progressed from something rigorous and daunting to something rather easy.

I survived the semester, and the payoff was grand. In May 1973, Margaret Hill and I walked the aisle of the Highland Presbyterian Church just down the street from the Hills' house. It was the most beautiful moment with the most beautiful woman I'd ever seen. We kissed under the instruction of a good and faithful minister and were pronounced Mr. and Mrs. John Paine. There was a reception with dinner and dancing, followed by a rice storm, followed by a three-day honeymoon in the big city of Dallas. It was simple, I suppose, but those were simpler times. It was perfect.

We returned to College Station, and I dove back into my studies. In a sink-or-swim program, things began to click. I honed my ability to visualize texts until my recall was almost instant. I earned high marks in calculus and physics. I set the curve in my accounting classes and excelled in engineering. My grades climbed. Everyone was astounded—Margaret as much as anyone—and the professors praised my efforts. This praise built my confidence but also stoked my need for further validation.

I was good enough.

I was smart enough.

I wasn't the slow one anymore.

Each semester, class ranks were posted, and by the midpoint of my junior year, a classmate came to me, offering his congratulations. "For what?" I asked, and he responded, "John, you're number two in the class." I was speechless. Nervous as I was about succeeding, about passing my classes, I never dreamed I'd be among the top students, and so had not checked the rankings. I hustled to the bulletin board where the standings were posted, and sure enough, there it was:

2. John Paine

By the spring semester of my senior year, the construction companies came calling. First, it was CECO Construction out of Chicago. They flew me to their home office in Chicago, wined and dined me, and handed me an envelope with a generous formal offer. Next, Chicago Bridge & Iron—a company that was not based in Chicago, did not build bridges, and never worked with iron—interviewed me, and they too made an exceptional offer. I had two birds in the hand, had succeeded in creating options for my future family. I was a coveted asset; companies wanted me. My self-confidence swelled. And with these top-tier job offers, with an expanded sense of self-worth, I returned home to meet with Mr. Hill.

I drove to the lake house on Lake Palestine, where Mr. Hill was already waiting. He knew I had some fine prospects and knew I'd considered forgoing these options to become a structural engineer. Armed with that information, he sat me down on the outdoor deck.

"Let's talk about your options. You're thinking about becoming an engineer?" he asked. But before I answered, he continued, "If you want to become an engineer, you can. But consider this. Would you rather be an engineer or have engineers work for you? If you come to work for me, we'll make sure they work for you."

I was an Aggie, yes, but his words made the decision easy. My potential future as a structural engineer evaporated.

"Even if I don't pursue engineering," I said, "I have some good job offers here."

I slid the letters across the table as if I held all aces, as if I had some leverage. Mr. Hill didn't even open the envelopes.

"You can take either of these jobs," he said. "You can go to work for one of these big outfits and be a small peg in a great big organization. You'll never learn the industry, though, not really. If you come to work for me, I'll teach you everything from project development to project delivery. I'll give you the opportunity to know everything there is to know about the industry."

He was sure of himself, as was Mr. Hill's way, but I knew he was right. I looked at the papers I'd slid across the table.

"Aren't we going to talk about compensation?" I asked.

He said, "Does it really matter what the compensation is? We both know I'm offering you the opportunity of a lifetime."

When I didn't respond, we both knew.

"When can you start?" he asked.

The opening ceremonies of the documentary premiere come to a close, and Josh takes the attendant controls of my wheelchair again. He steers me back down the ramp, back through the crowd, back down the hall, and into the theater that served as the greenroom for the prescreening reception. So many of the same friends are in that room, and they smile as I enter. Their eyes say it all—they approve of me; they appreciate me; they see me as a success, even in this immobile, incompetent state. There was a time when I needed this sort of affirmation, when I needed others to prop up my low self-worth. Now, it's an afterthought. I've learned the secret of validation.

I'm wheeled to an accessible spot on the first tier of the theater's stadium seating. Margaret sits to my right, Leo to her right. Behind me another man wheels in, and I can hear the whirring of his ventilator. He's received his ALS death sentence, too, perhaps only a year ago. We're in different stages of the same disease, the same breakdown, the same slow suffocation. But then again, I suppose everyone is in different stages of some similar disease. We're all making our way to the end.

The theater lights dim, and the screen is all aglow. I pray nothing but hope, grace, and that the people would see how learning to die has brought me to life. And this is life—to know that in my state of dependence and impairment, God is closer than the pain, closer than the air forced into my lungs, closer than the disease that so many count a curse, closer than my next thought. He is closer than all of these things, though it took me years of pain to learn this.

Dear God, speak to each person's heart as they watch this movie, I pray. *Let them learn to be one with you, even as we are one.*

PART II

The Errors

CHAPTER 7

A Tale of Two Paines

How did I come by my false identity, and how many years did I project it? I did my best to make others believe that I was John Paine, the competent, the sure-footed, the successful entrepreneur. Now I'm sitting on the floor level of a stadium-tiered theater, looking at another image projected on the screen. It's an exaggerated image of my own disability. My bust is—what?—forty-five feet tall? I am larger-than-life, each labored breath hissing at the crowd in surround sound. I am a reminder to this crowd: death comes for us all.

This footage was captured months ago, before ALS robbed my diaphragm of so much of its muscle tone. I watch the image of my former self. As difficult as it was in those days, I hadn't resorted to the round-the-clock use of the ventilator. Now, that danged nasal pillow is almost always shoved up my nostrils. I consider my present condition, listen to the rhythmic whir of the machine, the click and wheeze, click and wheeze. I feel my lungs fill and release on rhythm. The rhythm of the ventilator serves as a constant reminder of my coming suffocation. It's as inevitable as the ending of this movie, the snuffing of my life. All lives must come to an end. Even mine. I think the real pain of life is buried somewhere in that realization.

The supersized version of me speaks to the camera in rhythm with my waning breath.

"I would say my story is one of two John Paines," he says, then pauses. "First one is the normal guy that graduates from college and is married to his childhood sweetheart."

Pause.

"Enjoyed being a husband to my wife."

Pause.

"A father to my children. Truly felt like I had a pretty good life."

Josh's face takes the screen, and he tells the audience that I was the biggest of fathers, the consummate winner. Margaret speaks to the audience next, intimates that perhaps I was a workaholic. My business partners, Gary Wood and A. C. Musgrave, describe me as an exceptional businessman, maybe even one of the best. Praise, praise, praise—this is the kind of thing I lived for in the days before my diagnosis.

My image takes center screen again.

"There were a few things I was missing that I didn't want to tell anyone about."

Even in this documentary, there are things I didn't say, things I wish I would have now. Things like this: everything in my life looked so good, but I didn't really understand what it meant to have a meaningful relationship with God, Margaret, or my children. Or that my accomplishments and achievements somehow undermined authentic connection, true intimacy.

This is the right way to say it. Yes, I am the tale of two Paines. There were the best of times—those driven days of success and self-sufficiency.

I was on top of the world, a man with the Midas touch. But then came the worst of times, those days that brought the painful unraveling of my ego. How can a life swing from one extreme to the next? I suppose it's not as uncommon a story as so many might expect, at least not before the ALS diagnosis.

For the sake of clarity, you should know this about my life: if the early years of my journey were a slow slog of embarrassment and ineptitude, my adult years represented a reversal of fortune. I was the slow kid growing up, the dim lightbulb of the Paine family. I was the odd-bodied adolescent with the poor eyesight. I'd never been enough for my father, had never measured up. When recognized for anything, it was for my mediocrity. When praised for anything, it was for managing to avoid abject failure. All emotions were mocked. Every failure was highlighted. But in my college years and into adulthood, things changed. I was a man of momentum, a shooting star. I was the able-bodied one who'd managed to marry the gorgeous girl from Tyler. In childhood I was the punch line for many jokes. In adulthood I became the solution to many problems. I believed there were no limits to what I could achieve, but how does self-confidence skyrocket even when self-image remains in the basement? I was an embodied contradiction.

In 1975 I joined Mr. Hill's commercial construction company as a job site superintendent. My first assignment was managing the construction of a small office building for the oil and gas giant Exxon. I planned ahead and thought through every task days in advance. I did what I could to make sure each crew had what they needed to optimize each day's tasks. As a result of my careful planning, I delivered the project months ahead of schedule and saved one-third of the labor budget, which doubled the projected profit on the project. Mr. Hill was, of course, pleased. In thirty years, no one had ever doubled the profit on a project, and he compensated me well.

It became apparent that I could manage a profitable project, and I could still swing a hammer with the best of them, but I wasn't content with this sort of ground-floor perfection. I wanted to climb the ladder to the top. So, I poured myself into my work, hoping that by my training, a growing self-confidence, and the application of an insatiable drive, I might be recognized. I seized every opportunity to streamline a business process, control costs, and increase the profits on any given project. I exerted more and more control over the business, hoping that I might leave my thumbprint on the most profitable projects.

Under my watch, the profitability of the company increased. I had become Mr. Hill's proverbial golden goose. Our clients knew my name, knew my skills. The praise came, and the money followed. I worked longer and longer hours, always building, always reaching for the next rung of the ladder of success. As I climbed, and climbed, and climbed, I looked around. Was anyone matching my pace? Wasn't I the best and brightest up-and-comer? Wasn't I smart, capable, even exceptional?

Mr. Hill's profitability grew, and as it did, my bank accounts grew. I searched for validation there too. I was on my way to providing Margaret with the very lifestyle she'd grown accustomed to in her earlier years. But here, I found the first cracks in my porcelain identity. Why didn't she praise our shared financial success? Why didn't she praise me for the stability I was creating for her? Was I not enough for Margaret?

I pushed back the questions, the emotions that might indicate a problem. I set my sights on the next achievement, the next success. The altitude of achievement can be so distracting, so intoxicating.

I reached the top of Hill Construction Company and took a good look around. I was the man in control, second only to Mr. Hill. I was Joseph in Mr. Hill's Egypt, the governor of the granaries of the region's largest construction company. But did Joseph thirst for more, as I did? Did he still want the approval of his brothers, his father, even while he was a functional pharaoh?

It was 1983, eight years after I'd graduated from Texas A&M, when my fourth child entered the world. We had everything we'd wanted—a full family, financial stability, a nice home. By all outward appearances, things were going well, but I can look back on those days and see a man flailing, trying to prove himself. I carried so much unrest. And so, even with the success of Mr. Hill's company under my management, even with the praise of so many and my swelling bank account, my need to prove myself was unquenched. The truth as I saw it was simple: I was only managing the company Mr. Hill had built.

Mr. Hill was more like a father than an employer, and as with any father-son relationship, I suppose, there comes a day when the young buck needs to make his own way. I wanted my own company, one that offered me complete control, complete ownership. So, after eight years on the job and no small amount of discussion with Margaret, I left Don Hill Construction Company and created my own company, Client Construction Management.

I set about to carve out a niche for myself in the Texas construction industry and pioneered a new technique that I called "value engineering." I sold potential clients on the idea, showed them how employing my expertise from the earliest stages of the project would lead to substantial cost savings, and ultimately, greater profitability. I pounded the concrete, ginned up business for my young company, and in time, I developed a relationship with the Trammell Crow Company, one of the largest developers in the United States. And this account was the spring-board for instant success.

I oversaw the construction of commercial buildings, schools, indus-trial complexes, office complexes, and churches for Trammell Crow and others. I built, and built, and built, and in only a few short years, I'd created a very profitable business.

I'd created.

I'd achieved.

Recognition poured in from everywhere. I was named the president of the Northeast Texas chapter of Associated General Contractors of America. I became the president of the local Rotary Club and the local American Red Cross chapter. I became a go-to adviser and board mem-ber for various businesses, nonprofit boards, and community service projects.

The recognition scratched some deep itch, but never for long. Somehow, it all felt so hollow, so empty. Why did I keep coming back to the haunting questions?

When will it ever be enough?

When will I ever be content?

Drive more. Push more. Build more. Shore up the identity. I thought these might provide a solution for my season of discontent. But here's what they don't tell you about success—it cannot bring healing to your hidden wounds. It never quenches your thirst for more. It cannot val-idate you. Instead, it promises only hollow vindication. It puts words in our mouths—*I'll show them* or *Look at me*—then prods and prods and prods us to push past hidden pain. In the end, none of the success brought me what I hoped it would. Instead, it left me wanting more, and in that search for more, I'd sacrifice relationships with the people dearest to me. What's worse? I was oblivious to it all.

You should also know this: I knew how to create the most beautiful facades on any commercial building. And I was well acquainted with creating spiritual facades in my personal life. Sure, my spiritual life was dry, but couldn't I outwork the pillars of my church, the Bible study leaders, the fellas in my men's groups? Couldn't I be a well-polished Christian? Wouldn't God reward my hard work, all my attempts at holiness?

By my mid-thirties, I had a solid grasp on the Scriptures. I'd learned every right religious answer, and I wielded those answers with Texas-sized confidence. My young family was at every service, dressed in their Sunday best and smiling. I taught Sunday school classes that grew and grew until they overflowed any given classroom space. But I wasn't just respected for my devotion to attending every service or my ability to teach. My tithes and offerings caught the eye of the pastor too. And because I'd learned the leadership skills of business, because I was recognized as a go-to fella in commerce, I assumed the same sort of role in church. I was a deacon. I chaired committees. I was important.

I had done the things good Texas Christians do: I had asked Christ to come into my life and take charge; I'd attended church, given generously, served faithfully; I didn't swear, didn't drink; I was a model of moral purity; I spent daily time in Bible study and prayer. I'd done my best to avoid God's judgment, his critical eye, and by all measures of comparison, I was doing better than others around me. I outworked the lot of them, showed I could out-serve, out-give, and outperform. I worked so hard to please the only God I knew—God who was like my father; God the great accountant, the great judge; the fearsome, grand God; God who required me to clean up before coming into his presence. But with all this work, all this cleaning up, why did I sense I was always a little on the debit side of God's accounting ledger? Why wasn't God showing up for me? Why wasn't he close?

The voices kept haunting—*More, more, more, you must do more.*

I pushed the questions and fears back, and back, and back, and I pushed into more study, more knowledge. I tried harder and harder to get it right. I polished my image a little more, upped the starch in my shirts. I controlled my appearance, controlled the narrative—*John Paine is a good Christian and a godly man.* Wasn't this a grand identity? Cinching the knots of my ties tighter, I failed to realize I was only tightening the hangman's noose. I was suffocating, and I didn't even know it.

I was known and respected as a stand-up Christian, someone who served and loved his Lord, and I suppose that was true in part. Here was the whole truth: service, I knew; love, I did not. What did it mean to love the Lord? What did love mean at all? Is love really love if it doesn't produce the fruit of true intimacy? What was intimacy, anyhow?

I didn't know how to ask these questions back then.

You could have asked me how I felt about God in those days, and who knows what I would have said. I might have given you an answer straight from Scripture, might have recited it with robotic eloquence. But if you had asked about my heart's connectedness with God, I would have stood silent.

What am I missing?

What is the heart?

Can a man even know it?

———※———

Know this about my marriage: I'd learned to build facades there too. What appeared so perfect was little more than good theater. Margaret and I had the picture-perfect story—high school sweethearts, virgin-married, four children, the right house in the right neighborhood. We'd been in love from the beginning, but in the middle stretch of our marriage, we were finding that sometimes love doesn't cut it. Sometimes love isn't enough. At least not the love we knew then.

As more and more opportunity came my way, I discovered the power of the ego—it felt good to be important. Importance scratched my itching need for validation, at least for a moment. And as I began to buy the myth of my own heroism, my own importance, a sneaky sort of arrogance seeped into our marriage. I was the one with the ability. I was the one with the answers. I knew the path forward. And even if this wasn't always the case, I could control every aspect of my life to leave that appearance—even my marriage.

I suppose it's worth mentioning that in those days Margaret and I were members of more theologically conservative churches, churches that taught a woman's godliness was marked by her submissiveness. We attended church-recommended conferences—conferences by those such as Bill Gothard—that taught women were ever under the authority of their husbands. Wives should bring all questions about the Bible to their husbands and were not allowed to teach boys over the age of twelve. Wives were taught to submit to all their husbands' decisions. They were instructed to shelter under the cover of their husbands' all-knowing, ultramasculine, God-shaped wisdom regardless of the circumstances. It was a submissiveness that said Margaret could not be who she was. And even if that was not the explicit teaching of the churches, it was the way we interpreted too many messages.

Margaret was a spunky, strongheaded wife, but she wanted to be the godly woman of Scripture. So, she tried her best to fit into the mold. She began to withhold her opinions, and the spark of her youth waned. She bent to my growing arrogance and accepted my attempts to control the narrative. She conformed, retreated into the shadows, even as I elevated the reputation of John Paine higher and higher. And as she retreated and I pushed ahead, what had once been a life-giving relationship was turning cold.

The growth of my business, our financial security, my status in the church and community—none of it cured our marital difficulties. In fact, the more I accomplished, the more distant she became. I didn't want Margaret to lose her spark, nor did I want her to become more submissive. I wanted her to be assertive, so long as she asserted that I was enough for her, that I mattered. So, I pressed harder, but instead of merely becoming assertive, she became critical and negative. More and more, she pointed out my failures and flaws, the ways I wasn't measuring up. So, I tried harder to measure up even more. I took more calls at home, talked more about my successes and accomplishments. I hoped she might see just how important I was, and so often, I'd look across the table, searching for the look that said, *You're doing such good work, John.* Instead, I was met with a different sort of look—*When are you coming home, John?* And as the years passed, even that look changed—*I don't even care anymore*, her eyes said.

Maybe Margaret just wanted more of my time. Maybe she wanted to believe she mattered to me as much as the appearance of things mattered. Maybe she just wanted me to give up control. Maybe she wanted partnership. Who knew? I didn't.

I couldn't see past my own need to control my image in those days. I couldn't see that the more I fought to perpetuate a false identity of perfection—the look of success—the less intimate we were becoming. This is what attempts to control do, I suppose: they isolate us from those who don't want to be controlled.

The years churned on, and Margaret and I did what so many couples do. We adapted, made do with the relationship we had. I continued to grow my construction company and invested in a consumer products company on the side. I turned the crank on the family mint's printing presses, loading our bank accounts with cash. Margaret tended to the children, dutiful as she was. We moved to a new home in Dallas so I could be closer to my business interests, which were demanding more and more of my time. We drove the family car to church, put on the happy face, and pretended that everything was just so. We never fought in front of the children; in fact, we didn't fight much at all. Instead, we *coexisted*—Margaret with my controlling perfectionism, and I with her criticism, withdrawal, and silence. And though we would have both said we were best friends, though we would have both meant it, a great distance was growing between us. I could feel the void setting in.

The great void of communication.

The great void of connection.

The great void of intimacy.

This is how the black hole of a marriage widens, even when both want nothing more than intimacy.

In the summer of 1990, we made a last-ditch effort. We sat in straight-backed chairs in a marriage therapist's office. Margaret told her side of the story, and I told mine. The details aren't worth recounting except this one: neither of us was able to see the other's point of view. I was convinced that Margaret was plumb crazy. I'm sure she thought the same of me. Session after session, therapist after therapist, we tried to find a solution, but we couldn't find common ground; instead, we pointed fingers.

This story, it seemed, was writing itself to an inevitable conclusion. We would wait for the kids to graduate. After that, all bets were off. Still,

I gussied up for the community, for the local church, for my friends. I continued to promote the false image of John-Paine-the-Competent, hoping no one would discover what I know now—I was a dead man walking.

Dead man walking—if only I had known how freeing that truth might become.

CHAPTER 8

Who's in Control?

There's a story being told tonight, and it's the story of my disease mixed with inspiration, the ways I've refused to give up and die. That's only part of the story, though. There's a fuller story, a more complicated narrative vein.

The images flash across the screen. Footage from a Christmas home video recording. There is Margaret, smiling, even though I know our marriage is unraveling. There is Hillary, a teenager, stick thin and also smiling, but I know she is unraveling too. By all outward appearances, she is happy-go-lucky. She is not quite a child but not yet a woman. She is somewhere in between. You can see her mother's moxie on the screen; her father's headstrong willfulness sleeps somewhere just below the surface. She didn't fall far from either tree. This, I guess, is why pain became her lot. She came by it honestly, just like all the Paines, just like the rest of humanity.

These middling years were the hardest for Hillary, though you couldn't have guessed it from the video. She'd already learned to project a false self, a self that would jibe with the familial image I demanded. She was only just in her teenage years, and already she knew the game. She'd watched me play it for years.

In those years, I was a firm believer in the illusion of control. Control the business, control the dollar, control the time, control the image; the narrative—control, control, control. Only by control can you keep the things that might hurt you at arm's length—things such as histories, rejection, and emotions. Only by control can you hide the fear and protect the self-image you are selling. I didn't recognize it in those days, but the testimony of my life spoke the truth, if only I had listened.

Lack of self-awareness doesn't change the truth, does it?

God is a master interventionist. How often does he undo everything in one fell swoop? Is it his way to bring our complexes to a screeching halt? Does he often allow the bleak midwinter without days of preparation, without the warning of the autumn months? I suppose it happens—nature isn't always a perfect representation of life—but my experience is, I suppose, more akin to the natural order. God's grace is so often gentle. It operates along progressions. Every epiphany is preceded by a smaller epiphany, which feels like *the* epiphany. Every smaller epiphany is preceded by an undoing, an unbecoming. This, I think, is what we mean when we talk about the grace of God. This is what happened to me in my midlife years.

We were on the slippery slide to marital dissolution in those days, though you'd have never known that by the way we carried on in public. We were scratching and clawing, holding on to the scraps of our relationship, when we noticed something curious. Our fourteen-year-old daughter, Hillary, was losing weight, and this was not the weight loss of a girl trying to trim up. Hillary was built on a slight frame and had always been thin. Now she was transforming into a skeleton.

In July of Hillary's fourteenth year, Margaret was walking past the bathroom when she heard a gagging sound from the other side of the cracked door. Concerned, she peeked inside and found Hillary bending over the toilet, finger down her throat. Margaret pulled her away from the toilet and did what any mother blindsided by a bulimic episode might do—she told her to stop it, for good.

Hillary was the strongest willed of our children, but she was so good. She earned high grades at school and excelled at cheerleading, dance, and gymnastics. She was a well-liked girl, popular among her friends. Though she was strong-willed—just like me—she lived for her parents' praise, and in the past, if either of us gave her instruction, she listened—at least, most of the time. But in the days following the discovery of her eating disorder, something shifted. We never caught her purging again—at least not outright—but she continued to shed pounds. Food, she said, tasted metallic if it tasted at all, and she refused to eat. At supper, her fork pushed peas around the plate or her plate sat untouched, and across the table I watched in disbelief.

"This is what Paines do," I chided. "We eat our food. We take care of our bodies. We do what we need to do to be the best we can be." I didn't realize it at the time, but weren't these words of control, of performance? Though it is true that I loved my daughter and wanted her to be healthy, I also didn't want her to tarnish the family image. We were the Paines—performers, achievers, self-sufficient, successful in whatever we set our minds to. We were competent. We had solutions, not problems. And here came Hillary, threatening to undermine that image.

Hillary became more obstinate, and I watched as her paper-thin skin seemed to stretch across her delicate collarbones. I watched as she lost ten pounds, then twenty, then thirty. And it wasn't just the weight loss that was so concerning. She'd been a charismatic girl. She was an extrovert, a social butterfly, the life of every party. But now, she refused to leave the house, especially if a boy would be around. She became more and more withdrawn. She was receding into a darkness, but what darkness? Who knew?

I thought I could push her to eat; I thought I could make her eat. I thought I could control the stubbornness out of her, maybe thought I could bend her into the shape of success. But Hillary's eating disorder didn't grow from rebellion. It grew from something else. It grew from secrets and shame, and how could she confess secrets to her perfect, in-control father? How could she ruin the put-together family image by sharing her own brokenness?

The projection of perfection held my daughter's pain at arm's length. Her secrets and shame held intimacy with me at arm's length too.

False image, secrets, shame—these are the altars where intimacy is sacrificed.

———— ✕ ————

At our collective wits' end, we took Hillary to a local church counselor, hoping to find the root of her struggle. Was it spiritual? Was it something else? Weeks passed, then months. That's when I received the telephone call from Margaret.

"Hillary's therapist called," she said. "She wants to see us."

A few days later, we sat in the counselor's office on an overstuffed couch. The office was spacious and well-appointed with modern furniture. Degrees lined the creamy walls. Margaret and I sat on one side of a desk; the counselor sat on the other, arms crossed and leaning in.

"Your daughter struggles with depression," she said, and in an instant, I struggled to find traction. Hillary was depressed? Hillary, the kid with the infectious smile? The life of the party?

Before I found a grip, she sent the next volley across the desk.

"She also struggles with a severe eating disorder, and this, I fear, is outside of my area of expertise."

Margaret turned to me and grabbed my hand. She squeezed. These things—they weren't computing.

"But there's a reason for her eating disorder. She's in great pain. She feels out of control, and eating is one area she feels she can exert great control. Do you follow?"

I didn't, but I nodded.

"Hillary has given me permission to share this with you. When she was a little girl, she was molested."

There was the root.

The counselor continued, telling us that so often anorexia and bulimia operate like addiction. The false control it promises can be a distraction from the pain, at least for a while.

"Your daughter needs treatment," she said.

I knew she was right. The months that followed were some of the most painful of my life. We took Hillary to doctors and therapists. Severe as her eating disorder was, she'd suffered heart damage. And try as we did to steer her into health and wholeness, she would not comply. Perhaps she could not comply. Between learning about Hillary's disease, researching outpatient eating-disorder facilities, and trying to keep her alive, Margaret and I exhausted ourselves. We were running out of options when we found Remuda Ranch, a facility specializing in pediatric eating disorders. On little more than a set of airline wings and a prayer, we flew our youngest daughter to Arizona in hopes of finding the help she needed.

After leaving Hillary at Remuda Ranch, we returned to Dallas, falling into bed. Margaret looked at me and said, "I'm not sure I can take it anymore."

This life, this image of perfection, this illusion—was it evaporating? Why did I feel like such a failure?

Hillary's eating disorder was gut-wrenching, life altering. It was the most difficult of situations. And as it wore on, as it exposed the ways I wasn't in control of my family, other failures came knocking.

What about my business? What about John Paine, the captain of commerce? The false narrative was being exposed there too. The real estate market had taken a nosedive in 1988, but thanks to a piece of timely advice, some good financial planning, and a proper hedge, I'd managed to avoid bankruptcy. As fortune would have it, just before the crash, the folks at Trammell Crow called. The market was shaky, they said, and they needed to cut all of my contracts loose. They were asking for a favor, and they'd owe me one, they said. I examined the options. I supposed I could sue them, but what would that get me? Each of the Trammell Crow projects I was involved with was on the verge of insolvency. The writing was on the wall.

The silver lining, I suppose, was that I'd managed to put money back during the good years, and I'd established quite the rainy-day war chest. In fact, I'd parlayed a tidy sum of that war chest into other investments, including the purchase of a consumer goods company, Excelex Corporation. So, with a real estate bust on the horizon and the value of my real estate holdings cratering, I deleveraged as quickly as I could. I walked away from the contracts I could and negotiated settlements on the balance. It was a painful extrication, but when the dust settled, I still had a tidy sum and my ownership interest in Excelex.

Before my Excelex play, I had no experience with the consumer goods manufacturing business. A review of the financial statements and business model, though, indicated there was potential for the company to make serious money if a few changes were made. It was a gamble, yes, but the gamble paid off. By the time the real estate crash had run its course, Excelex was practically printing cash. I'd read the data points correctly and visualized the kind of company Excelex could be, even without experience in the industry. Paine-the-Competent had become Paine-the-Turnaround-Artist, and year after year, I took healthy profits and stashed them away in case another rainy day should find me.

As profitable as Excelex was in the early 1990s, the mid-1990s proved to be another story. The chemical suppliers for Excelex convened at an industry trade show in the final quarter of 1995, and in an act of collusion, they doubled the prices of our raw materials. The price hike had an immediate impact, and in a matter of days, Excelex went from being a cash cow to a barren heifer. We bled cash for months and tried our best to right the ship, but there was no salvaging it. Defeated, my business partner and I made a hard call: we would liquidate the company.

These things happen in business. Markets ride high for a season and dry up in the next. Years of plenty give way to years of drought. This is why Mr. Hill always cautioned me to manage the years of plenty well, and the good news was, I had. I'd shored up our bank accounts through the prosperous years and had made other successful ventures. We were more than comfortable, and I even contemplated retiring in the wake of the Excelex debacle. So, why did these two business failures hurt so much? Why did I feel so empty, so crushed? Why was I considering withdrawing from business altogether?

Try as I might, I couldn't control the market cycles, the variables. Try as I might, I couldn't control my marriage, spiraling as it was into darkness. I couldn't control my daughter, who continued to push peas and potatoes around her plate, blithe to the sharpening of her cheekbones. I couldn't control God, with whom I was supposed to be growing closer.

The narrative was falling apart. The perfect image I'd tried so hard to project—the image of competency, godliness, self-reliance, and success—was tarnishing, rusting, perhaps disintegrating.

That's when the doubt came calling.

I can see it now, the way doubts come prowling like a monster. I see how they spring from false belief or unmet expectations. Hadn't I served God as best I knew how? Didn't God promise to provide for those who loved him, for those who did the right things in faith? Hadn't I done all the right things? Hadn't I outworked everyone? So, where was he? Did he see me? If he did, then why the failure of my businesses, of my marriage? Why wouldn't he intervene in Hillary's life; why wouldn't he make her eat? Shouldn't I reap the rewards? After all, without some reward, what good is rigorous dedication? What good is all of this faith? Even more, what of his promised comfort and closeness?

I distilled the questions until I was left with only two: *What is the benefit of serving a God who won't show up and intervene in the messes of your life?* And, *What's the difference between a God who can't show up and one who won't?* This kind of God—I questioned his goodness, at least toward me. All this work for him, and what had I gotten? Nothing but despair.

When the doubts solidify, when they take the form of an unsolvable equation, then what? There was no good answer, I supposed, and in my lack of a solution, this made the most sense: I'd withdraw from the God who had seemed to withdraw from me. I'd never stop believing, but I wouldn't keep pursuing either. If God wanted to keep his distance, I was happy to oblige.

It's been years since those doubts took shape, and here's what I can say looking back. It is God's grace that allows the sabotaging of our own self-reliance, our arrogant mechanisms of control. He crushes the false beliefs that lead us away from him. It is God's grace that sneaks up on all our doubts and buries them in the grave too. He has a way of shaking us free—if we're willing to be shaken, that is—and sometimes, he uses the people we least expect.

It was Margaret.

It was Margaret.

It has always been Margaret.

CHAPTER 9

Firing God

The narrative I'd tried so carefully to control was spinning away from me. The illusion of my competency and self-sufficiency was proving to be a highway mirage. The wells of validation I'd turned to—business, marriage, church, family—had all run dry. What was left?

In the fall of 1997, Hillary was in inpatient therapy for her eating disorder. I'd suffered the loss of two businesses. My marriage was contentious on the best of days. My spiritual life was lackluster, more of a duty than a labor of love. I wasn't undone—not just yet—but I was in the process of being undone, though I didn't know it then. I was blazing a trail into the disillusionment and apathy of middle age.

Margaret tore another trail. She got active. She saw how my attempts to fix every problem, to create the false image of the perfect Texas family, put everything off-kilter, and so, she made a decision. She was finished with the illusions and images. Someone needed to help Hillary in her recovery instead of trying to solve the problem by brute force or otherwise trying to whitewash it. That someone, she decided, would be her.

Unsure where to start, Margaret began to read recovery literature. She read and researched like a woman on a mission and began to understand the shame and fear that drove Hillary's sickness. Anorexia and bulimia, it turned out, are like any other addictive behavior; they are so often attempts to numb the pain of life. If she was going to help Hillary confront the pain of her abuse and kill the demons of shame and fear, she'd have to find a source of strength, and the fact was, I was in no position to lend her any.

Just months into Hillary's recovery, Margaret picked up a book written by the mother of a girl who struggled with bulimia. This mother had found the support she needed in Al-Anon, a group designed to help support family members of addicts. This was all the hope Margaret needed. She found a local Al-Anon group and became a faithful attender straightaway. They welcomed her and included her from the minute she walked in the room. They surrounded her with love and acceptance and compassion, the things she needed the most. They provided her with listening ears and helped carry the emotional baggage I could not. Margaret had only wanted to learn how to help our daughter live. In this group, though, she was finding her own way of new life.

In the early mornings, as I buttoned up my starched white shirts and knotted my power-red ties, Margaret sat in the quiet, reading her Al-Anon books. These books, she said, were a source of wisdom and strength, but I was unconvinced—at least, at first. Wasn't all this recovery stuff a bunch of feel-good pop psychology? Wasn't it for people who couldn't control their emotions, who lacked willpower, who couldn't muscle their way through adversity? Wasn't it just for addicts? Neither of us was an addict, so what good could all this recovery mumbo jumbo do for either of us? I knew we needed help, sure. I doubted this was it, though.

I suppose I wasn't ready for recovery, not at first. I clung white-knuckled to the image of my success, even though that image was tarnished at the moment. In the later stages of my ALS, I've come to know that releasing the false image of success and self-sufficiency means confronting haunting questions, questions such as this one: *Am I enough?* And to confront that question—to really deal with it—I'd have to feel it. I'd have to get in touch with my emotions. I'd have to get vulnerable. I had no framework for this sort of deep healing work in those days, so I did what I knew best: I buried myself in work.

The months passed, and I sensed a softening in Margaret. I first noticed it when Hillary returned from Remuda Ranch. If she refused to eat, Margaret wouldn't show frustration or anxiety. Instead, she'd turn to Hillary with the kindest eyes, and with the patience of the best mother, she would remind Hillary, "This is not my disease." Margaret loved, and loved, and loved, and she did not let Hillary's willful refusal to eat hinder that love. When Hillary ate, she loved. When she refused to eat, Margaret loved anyway. And when I attempted to control Hillary or force her to eat, when I prepared an eating contract for her to sign that laid out my expectations, Margaret came to me in private. This was Hillary's burden to sort out, she said, not my problem to fix. But even in this, her tone had changed. There was no hint of criticism or negativity. It was different. She was sharing the advice she'd learned in Al-Anon, and she was doing it in a loving and accepting way. She was loving me as I was, just as she was loving and accepting Hillary as she was.

I watched Margaret change, saw her imbued with a quiet self-confidence, and it wasn't the self-confidence that came from striving for achievement. Instead, it was the self-confidence that came from a deeper well, from knowing herself, from experiencing some sort of salvation. No matter how Hillary struggled, no matter how I intervened, controlled, or judged, Margaret let it all roll off her back. Even when I goaded, Margaret remained calm and patient. She came out of the shell of her feigned submission and refused to withdraw. Negativity became a thing of the past. She was responsible for her own well-being, she told me, and nothing I did could change that. I watched as Margaret released the burden of fixing her daughter or our marriage, as she stepped into the quiet and peace-filled confidence, and I took notice. There was something stirring.

Some evenings, Margaret would invite me to sit with her and listen to a few passages from her Al-Anon materials. I balked at first, but over time, I was so attracted to the new Margaret that I wanted what she had. So, I sat and listened to the bits she might share. There were passages about peace, about validation. There were passages such as this one from *One Day at a Time in Al-Anon*:

> Every human being has his own individual drives and motivations, beyond my understanding and control. I may say: "But he *knew* what I *expected*," not realizing that it may have been precisely for this reason that he rebelled and acted otherwise.
>
> My search for peace of mind will bear fruit much more readily if I stop expecting and relax into acceptance.

The release of control and expectations, the falling into acceptance—these were foreign concepts to me. But reading along with Margaret, I began to understand that I'd foisted expectations on her and our family—project a perfect image, succeed, achieve. And when they couldn't live up to my expectations of perfection, I'd offered to "help" them, to fix the problem or save the day. Though I might have told you that all my attempts to help were born of love, if I'd have asked Margaret and the kids, they'd have said it all felt like so much control.

It was a slow awakening, but I began to see it. I'd bought into the hype—*John Paine can fix anything.* I examined the way I was treating Margaret, the way I was always offering to help her organize her day, helping her achieve maximum efficiency, or giving her the best route to any destination so she'd be five minutes early. I offered her mothering advice, saying, "The children might respond to you better if you just . . ." I looked at her recipes, offered to innovate the process to make it easier. I implemented family time-management skills that would help the children with their productivity and offered more effective ways for them to communicate their points. See my attempts to help? See the way they were born of my expectations? See how they looked like so much control? After all, without expectations, without control, how could I measure performance? How could I know whether I was worthy? Could I beat back the fears from my youth, the fears that were now taking shape in the wake of all my failures?

You are not enough.

You are not enough.

You will never be enough.

I suppose Margaret had her own expectations and her own ways of trying to control the outcomes before Al-Anon. She didn't expect perfection; she expected love—the pure, unconditional kind. So, when I lumbered in, offering to help or innovate or maximize, she'd become negative and angry, telling me my suggestions wouldn't work. If I pushed the issue, she withdrew, turned silent as a stone. She built a wall between us, one that was impenetrable. This was how she controlled me, how she guarded herself from my penchant for perfection.

Expectations and control—they wear so many masks. They sneak into any marriage. They build great walls too difficult to deconstruct, save for a miracle. This was the story of my own marriage. This was the story of my spiritual journey, too, though I hadn't realized it yet.

It was the dawning of a slow realization. I wasn't sure how to release my expectations or mechanisms of control, but here's what I did know: Margaret was finding her own path. She spoke of the love of God, how it was her source of validation and strength. He sat with her, like a close friend, she said. Her tenderness, her gentleness, even the firmness of her boundaries when I tried to control her or Hillary—all of it drew me in.

This was my first earnest taste of what an intimate relationship with God looks like. It's sinking into the knowledge that God loves you just as you are, that he doesn't expect perfection or the quantifiable metrics. He loves because he loves, unconditionally. This is the love Margaret was experiencing, and it was the love she was pouring into my life and into Hillary's. It was the love of a healthy, whole mother. It was the love of God.

In the evenings, Margaret and I walked our dogs and discussed the Al-Anon reading for the day. In the car, she'd read passages to me and I'd listen, soaking up the truths she'd already learned to take to heart. The days wore on. Hillary continued to struggle. And yet, I found that as Margaret loved me, I began to experience increasing peace as I followed her lead. The long winter of marriage was beginning to thaw, and there we were, enjoying each other again.

It's taken me years to understand the winter of our marriage. It wasn't as simple as I thought at the time. Margaret wasn't the problem, though she played a small part in our discord. She wasn't as crazy or negative as I thought. She didn't withdraw because she disliked me, but because my control and expectations got in the way of a healthy give-and-take. And though I loved my false image, my success and self-sufficiency, Margaret refused to see it, to tell me how great I was. She didn't care about any of that: the success, the money, the picture of perfection. She only wanted me. She wanted me without the performance routine. She wanted to see a glimpse of the boy she'd fallen in love with—the awkward, open, vulnerable boy from Tyler—and in those early years of discussing our Al-Anon readings, she made sure I understood that. What's more, she lived in a newfound freedom, a freedom from needing my affirmation, my approval. She was living secure, attached to the validation only God can give.

That new spring graced me with fresh eyes. If I could release my need for control, my expectations, and the metrics that offered false validation, maybe I could experience this kind of intimacy with God that Margaret enjoyed. Maybe I could build something authentic. But how?

<hr />

In the earliest days of a thawing heart, the ice still clings in the shadows. It's difficult to separate a man from his reputation, to peel the pride away. You can't unplug the false-image projector without blowing the bulb, or quit an addiction to external validation cold turkey. A man needs a slower way, a more secret way.

On the sly, I searched for an Al-Anon group that met during the workday. As luck or the hand of God might have it, there was a local group meeting at a quasi-convenient time, though it required a bit of a drive. I snuck out of the office over my lunch hour without leaving any indication of where I was heading. I pulled into a large upscale shopping center. There was a nondescript glass door, and I walked through, up a set of stairs, and into a spacious but bare room, chairs circled in the center. I took my seat among a diverse group of 12-steppers—some black, some white, some mothers, some fathers, some not quite adults. There were housewives dressed in their exercise clothes and a few men in business casual attire. These were not my standard lunch dates.

As we sat, I surveyed the crowd. What was I doing with such an odd group? Could I learn anything from a collection of folks, none of whom were titans of industry? But then, they spoke.

They confessed that they were powerless to control the uncontrollable—the addiction of their family members, their own addictions. They couldn't fix their loved ones, couldn't solve their problems. The confession of their weakness was astounding. This was not standard church talk by standard church folks; this was different, less certain, more broken. These people were able to articulate their emotions with clarity while I couldn't name what I felt in any given moment. They spoke of God, too, the ways they experienced him. God was not a set of data points to be summed; he was an intimate friend who could be trusted with anything.

Intimacy—was such a thing possible?

I'd sought intimacy with God my entire life, pursuing every imaginable avenue available. I was the most avid God hunter I knew, had pursued him as best I knew how. I spent hours in Bible study, quiet times, prayer, and Scripture memorization. I prayed and fasted. I'd been at the church every time the doors were open. I'd given more than 10 percent of my income to the church and was active on committees. I was active in gospel-centered nonprofit ministries. I'd expected that all this faithful service should somehow have resulted in the most powerful, most intimate relationship with God. So how was it that I'd not found what so many of these people had? How had so much brokenness, such a common lack of control, led them into what I'd wanted most—real relationship?

Perform, perform, perform—this had been my mantra. Do the right things, say the right things, believe the right things, have the right theology. But none of it seemed to help me draw God any closer. I supposed he must be too distant for me, or maybe he just didn't get involved. So, I'd done the only thing I knew—I'd controlled the narrative, whitewashed myself with an image of godliness.

I listened as many in this circle of new friends opened up about their lives. This intimacy they had, this relationship with God—could I have it too?

Little did I know that this sort of relationship was coming for me. But how are years of expectations, of validation seeking, of control mechanisms undone? What does it mean to walk into vulnerability? Could I ever admit I was powerless?

———✕———

The weeks and months continued to churn by, and I delved deeper into recovery. I delved deeper into Scripture, too, though it was with fresh eyes. It'd be a lie to say those groups shook me into an immediate experience of God, but day by day, I learned to release control and embrace my own powerlessness.

In the midst of my recovery, I was sharing about the doubts and pains of life with a dear friend, telling him how those doubts were starting to wane, though I couldn't express just why. I droned on for what must have been minutes before he stopped me.

"Have you considered your picture of God?"

I said nothing.

"How do you picture God? Really?"

I hesitated for a moment, searching for the right words. Did I know? Did I have a good answer?

Before I could drum something up, he looked at me and asked, "Does he look like an accountant?"

"I suppose. I guess I think he's always keeping score somehow."

He nodded, then followed. "Does he look like a judge sitting at the bench?"

"Maybe so. Isn't he the one who will be our ultimate Judge? Isn't he a little disappointed when we mess up?"

"Is your God critical of you? Do you have to clean yourself up in order to come before him?"

I considered it. Didn't he hate sin? Hadn't I been taught he couldn't be in the presence of filth, or moral decay, or the dirty? Shouldn't I try to bring the cleanest, best, most acceptable version of myself to him?

I didn't respond, but the astonished look on my face answered his questions. He stared me down and with the conviction of experience, said, "I think you need to fire your god and get another one."

Sacrilege.

Heresy.

But was it?

"Do you understand the complete concept of grace, John?"

I stared, blinking. I knew the definition of grace, had been taught it when I'd asked Christ to come into my life in junior high. I'd even taught it to so many others in small groups and Bible studies. But as I'd submitted to the instruction of the church, as I'd leaned into their definition of God, a wholly different god came into view. Doctrine by doctrine, tile by tile, piece by piece, my beliefs showed a mosaic of God the Accountant, God the Angry, God the Critical, God the Perfectionist, God the Judge, God the Disappointed, God the Distant. But God the Graceful? I guess I'd never quite experienced my heavenly Father that way, or my earthly father, for that matter. That's when it crystallized.

Earthly father to heavenly Father—somehow, I'd made them into conjoined twins. And so, as I'd tried to satisfy my earthly father's expectations by pushing down my emotions and trying my best to do things right, I'd done the same with God. I'd taken to satisfying him, to trying to clean myself up for him. I wanted only to be acceptable.

What fruit had sprung from my belief in this god of the ledger? Nothing but the failing works of my own self-sufficiency. Nothing but the false standards of success I'd judged myself by—the standard of my own perfection. I'd judged others by that standard too. In that judgment, hadn't I pushed intimacy away? I don't suppose anyone wants to be intimate with one who is constantly judging.

Grace—what was it, really?

"The God of grace loves you as you are, without condition," my friend said. "The God of grace says you matter, not because of what you accomplish, but just because. The God of grace wants to know you, the real you, without reservation. If I had to serve your god, I'd probably choose atheism instead."

Fire my god. I let the words rattle around. Such an easy thing to say, but such a hard thing to do after more than thirty years bowing down to the god of judgment and perfection. But my distorted reality—could it change if I didn't take some drastic measure? Had I damaged my relationship with God for good?

I wish I'd have understood the wisdom of the great theologian A. W. Tozer sooner, wisdom I'd heard but couldn't understand—"What comes into our minds when we think about God is the most important thing about us." I wish I'd have understood that my view of God influenced everything else—the way I acted, how I saw myself, the words I spoke, the way I treated others, the affirmation I sought. If I had, maybe I'd have righted the ship before I lost two businesses, almost a daughter, nearly a marriage, and maybe even myself. I suppose, though, that you cannot learn the hard lessons until the stuff of life robs you of your false notions, and life had only just become the robber.

I listened as he shared more about this God of unconditional love and grace, the God who wants nothing more than to be intimate with us. "Only God can help you rip through all these false ideas about him and the false ideas about your need to perform. Only God can give you a full understanding of real love, and only he can teach you what it means to find your identity in that love. You have to release control. All the way. Then you'll see it never really mattered anyway."

I didn't know what all this meant, but it seemed like the good news I'd been waiting to hear my whole life.

There are moments in life that need mining. There are hidden opportunities. You can place a Texas-sized wager, gamble big to buy the property, and get to digging. You can chicken out, too, and cluck your way back to the safety of life as you know it. But what if life as you know it isn't worth clucking back to? What if it's not working for you?

The challenge—fire my god—was my decision point. I took it and went all in. I suppose I've always had a bit of a gambler in me.

I pushed deeper and deeper into recovery and fired the old performance god as best I knew how. I murdered the god who was a disapproving father, the one wagging a finger and reminding me how inept I was. I did my best to bury the god who needed me to clean myself up, the one who required me to prove my validity by external metrics. I adopted the God of unconditional love, grace, and power, and somehow, I felt it past the bone. And in that I came to realize this: validation was an illusion; control was an illusion; false narratives, my false self, all of these falsities were illusions. My business, my bank accounts, my marriage, the attendance of the Bible studies I taught—did my attempts to find validation in any of these things bring me peace? Did they help me know God? The projection of my false self—the image of success I'd created—did it leave me fulfilled? Hardly.

The days passed. Then the weeks. I began to see how much healing I needed. I came to a vague, misty understanding—there could be no relationship with God if I didn't have a relationship with myself, my true self. Myself past my own standards, past my judgments. And who was I? How did I feel? What did it mean to feel?

I set out to understand my emotions—the anger, pain, and self-doubt that seemed buried so deep. More than anything, I wanted to understand how I—John Paine the slow, dim-witted, awkward-bodied boy from Tyler—could be fully known, fully loved, and fully validated by God. This was the earnest beginning of my recovery, the beginning of the transformation of my heart. This was the beginning of a journey to intimacy, and it came with little time to spare. Within months I'd be diagnosed with ALS.

CHAPTER 10

The Study

I've learned to be present in the moment over these last fifteen years (distraction isn't the best option when every breath matters), and tonight I'm trying my best to be fully present. I can feel the heaviness of the crowd gathered here. Many of these people have known me for years; this much is true. But have they taken the time to journey into the weight of my disease until tonight? I suspect they have not.

I hear sniffs in the room, notice the women in front of me pulling tissues from their purses. A man clears his throat. Just then, the screen fades from a still photo of Lou Gehrig, the baseball player who brought ALS into public consciousness, to Dr. Jeffrey Elliott, the director of the UT Southwestern ALS Clinic. Dr. Elliott explains the disease, and the air grows even thicker.

"It's progressive, and it's characterized by involvement of the motor neuron cells . . ."

Involvement. That's one way to put it. Over these last years, nearly every motor nerve cell in my body has died.

"It leaves people with weakness, with muscle atrophy, with trouble moving, with stiffness. It can start very subtly, with a little trouble lifting the foot or weakness in the hand, with slurring of the speech, trouble swallowing. It's a progressive disorder. It starts with very mild symptoms, and over time, of course, it becomes more severe."

The screen cuts from Dr. Elliott to my oversized bust, and this supersized image of me recounts the initial reaction to the diagnosis.

"Wow, that couldn't be me. Not going to happen. Not going to happen."

But it was me. It was happening. Nothing could stop any of it.

Disease is no respecter of persons. It does not choose the less-skilled, less-polished victims. It does not single out the less fit. Disease is not so Darwinian. Disease is the ghost that haunts some and not others. It is chance. It is the green zero on the roulette wheel; we are the silver ball.

I watch as Margaret's beauty radiates from the screen now, and she tells the audience that the prospect of losing me was insurmountable in those first moments after the diagnosis. Next, my children take turns lamenting those first days of the diagnosis, how hopeless and lost they felt. The prospect of losing someone you love before their time is its own sort of grief; the waiting for that loss is an even different sort of grief. All this grief, even before the dying is done.

I think about Margaret's words, about the children's. I consider my grandchildren, how they will lose a grandfather too early. ALS is a multi-headed parasite; it feeds on the hosts, sure, but it feeds on their families' lives too. For so many years I hadn't given much thought to my family's emotions. How can you consider the emotions of others when you can't even consider your own? I'm well acquainted with my emotions these days, and I'm reminded of that as the tightness in my gut releases, as the lump forms in my throat, as my cheeks warm and my eyes fill with tears.

Tears—I hate them, and it's a hatred not born of some supermasculine toughness. Tears, like so many other things, complicate my life. They build in the corners of my eyes, fill the rims. As the air from my ventilator backflows upward and through my tear ducts, it dries out the tears, leaving burning salt deposits.

Burning, stabbing, thudding, tearing, pulling, suffocating—these are the sensations of my slow death.

My eyelids are one muscle group I can still control, and now, I'm grateful I can pinch them closed. The relief is instant. I suppose Leo notices my eyes pinched shut, notices the tears squeezing from the sides, because I feel him wiping my cheeks, then dabbing the corners of my eyes. He's anticipated the need. Sometimes I wonder whether he knows me as well as I know myself.

I look back at the screen, but I'm not thinking so much about the documentary. I'm thinking about the day that parasite attached itself to our family. I remember that doctor's office, remember thinking how unfair it all was. That was the day I lost control in earnest. And this loss of control would be complete.

In the wee hours of my first day as an ALS patient, I lay in my bed, blinking. The muscles in my forearm twitched to the rhythm of death, a reminder of the way my life span had been compressed.

You will die.

You will die.

You will die.

I'd read about the stages of grief, the way one who's suffered any life trauma experiences anger before transitioning to denial. Denial gives way to bargaining with God. Depression follows, and sometimes accept-ance. I'd watched colleagues and partners walk through these stages when their business failed. I'd heard the stories from those who'd lost spouses and children, or who'd been diagnosed with cancer. Cognition and experience, though, are two very different things, and my midnight experience was this: those stages—save for acceptance—seemed to coexist. My life was as compressed and lifeless as the gray Dallas clay—Texas gumbo, we called it in my building days. So much for retirement, for enjoying this new and blossoming relationship with the wife of my youth. So much for holding my grandchildren. So much for so many things. The reaper was coming, and the harvest wasn't ready.

I blinked and found myself in denial.

How could this happen to me?

I blinked and discovered I was bargaining with God.

Haven't I been faithful? Please reverse this diagnosis; take this cup from me, and I'll be even more faithful.

I blinked, and the great weight of depression set in. There it was, the darkness of death—it had come calling for me.

It was a tornado of feelings I was not ready to experience. And what of the acceptance, what of hope and peace? What of the closeness of God, who comforts his children? The room was silent as a tomb.

The muscles in my forearm continued to twitch to the rhythm of the second hand passing, passing, passing me by.

I left Margaret to her own midnight tossing and turning and made my way to the study. I sat at my desk, surrounded by the library of books I'd collected over the years to validate my intellect. My computer stared at me, lifeless. There were to-do lists, itineraries, and account statements on that computer, the data to prove that I'd been a success. I pushed away Bible study notes, prayer lists, all the proofs of my can-do spirituality. All these things were reminders that my life had culminated in—*what?* None of it mattered now.

And this is when I did the very thing I'd not yet dared to do. I sat, fully examined all of my emotions, and I lashed out at God.

I've worked so hard, overcome so much.

I built wealth and gave so much of that money to you.

I've led Bible studies. Prayed with men who were losing their wives, their businesses, their minds.

I've served, and I've served, and I've served, and when you showed me that so much of my service was for the purpose of filling my own need for validation, I turned back. Over these last months, I've tried to find my validation and worth only in you. Don't you see how hard I've tried, how faithful I've been? How could you let this happen to me?

To me.

This kind of thing happens to other people, not me.

For an hour I felt it all; I spat it all. I might have cursed. I left no word unsaid. I pounded the desk with my fist. I couldn't help it. And when I thought I'd given God the best piece of mind the created had ever given the Creator, I sat, breathless.

There was silence for a moment. That's when the still, small voice came.

Are you done yet?

It echoed in a place I hadn't known existed. It was an interior place. The mind? No. The soul? I'm not sure. The heart? Yes, perhaps that was it.

I second-guessed the voice at first, but then I considered it. This wasn't something I'd say to myself. After all, I didn't want to be finished. I wanted to spill more words, to remind God of all the inequities of my diagnosis. I listened for it again, and sure enough, there it was. This time, though, I noticed the tone. There was not a hint of anger; it was not a scolding voice. It was not the condescending tone of a know-it-all father. Instead, it was pure love.

Really. Are you done yet?

I supposed.

I closed my eyes and seemed to be transported from my body. I saw myself as if through a window, saw the white knuckles of my folded hands and the way my shoulders sagged under too much weight. I saw the twitch in my forearm, saw my head bowed over the desk. There were tears on that desk. Had I been crying? I looked at the shell of my body, how it was illuminated only by the streetlight that came filtering through the window, and that's when the words began falling.

They fell less like rain and more like leaves in the dead of autumn. There were hundreds of them, the words that described my life falling, and falling, and falling down around me. Business deals. Partnerships. The names of people I was working with. The word *home* floated down, then all the numbers of my bank accounts, accompanied by every asset I owned. *Lake house* floated down, then flipped, and flipped again. There were the names of my children—*John, Josh, Amanda, Hillary.* Margaret's name came last, and it fell to the desk where the other words had piled. I had sped through the summer of my life and was standing in the autumn, and there were all the things I thought might give me life piled under my bowed head.

It was an unexpected vision, a vision that made no sense. And just when I considered dismissing this little trick of the mind, I felt a gust of wind, and the leaves of my life blew from the desk. In that same inner room, the quiet place—*my heart?*—I heard the voice again. This time I knew it was my heart. I felt it there, somehow, like whatever comes before love.

Nothing will ever be on the tabletop of your life again. Just me.

Looking back, I don't suppose it was as much of an admonition or command. Instead, it was a declaration, a statement that my God would come to me, would make himself known to me. I didn't understand that then, though.

I think I've got it now, Lord. It's just you and me from this day forward.

There was sorrow—how I'd searched for worth and validation in so many things other than God, how I thought those other things could somehow help me measure up. I'd only just begun to understand this when the diagnosis came screaming into my life. Then came confession—I'd misplaced my dependency; I'd attached myself to many other things. Next followed agreement—my priorities would be different from now on. That's when the love came—the deepest, gentlest, most unfathomable love. It was unlike anything I'd ever experienced.

I would fall apart; this much was true. I would be unable to perform the way I had for so long. I would have very little to offer in the way of skill, ability, stamina, or longevity of life. Still, I knew that God loved me. He loved me for me, not for what I could accomplish. He wanted to spend time with me more than he wanted me to accomplish anything for him. For what seemed like an hour, he allowed me to sit in that loving acceptance, to sink into it. This was a closeness I'd never felt—a real, tangible presence. Then, after the long, loving silence, the voice spoke again.

Reach down and pick up one of the names.

I stuck my spirit hand into the pile and retrieved Margaret's name. I walked to the desk and began to lay her name on the table when the voice came again.

Not there, John. Pull up a chair.

I pulled out the side chair from my desk, the one next to my bowing self, and the voice said, *Put Margaret in the chair.* And so I did.

Nothing will come between us again, not even Margaret. Nothing will validate you except me. Nothing will compete with me.

Had she been competing with God? Even from the early days of my faith, hadn't I believed that God was first, that not even Margaret was before him? Hadn't I said those words so many times before?

Words, words, words—they were all just words.

As if there was too much light in too dark a room, I couldn't see at first. But as I sat in that epiphany, I realized it—I'd let too much of the stuff of earth compete with God, even Margaret. I'd pushed God into smaller and smaller spaces as I let my ego fill larger and larger spaces. There was more sorrow. More confession. It was followed by more of that deep, abiding sense of unconditional love, the love that I'd done nothing to deserve.

There was Margaret's name, blinking in that chair. The still, small voice directed me to the rest of the words, and one at a time, I picked each up. But even as I reached for the leaves, the material stuff, the business deals, the partnerships and bank accounts, they each seemed to evaporate. I was left with only the names of my children and the names of friends who were most important in my life. I put those things in the chair and looked. It was a small stack of the most important things in life—people—and none of it went on the desk. That was the primary position, the place saved only for God. It was clear. I was to learn intimacy with God first, and in that intimacy with God, he'd pour his love into me. As I learned to live into this love, as I allowed him to pull back all the false layers of my own life, I'd find intimacy with others. And what of the money, the accounts, the stuff of earth? Its importance was somewhere down the line, if at all.

In an instant, I was back in my body, sitting at my desk, and that same voice began speaking Scripture over me. But it was Scripture spoken like I'd never heard. The words weren't stale, didn't sound as if they were being read from the pages of some preacher's Bible. There was no call to word study, to get to the root of the original languages for the purpose of teaching. The Scriptures washed over me, promises meant for my sustenance in this coming season of disability—*take and eat.*

- "I will never leave you nor forsake you." (Heb. 13:5 NKJV)
- "I will ask the Father, and he will give you another advocate to help you and be with you forever." (John 14:16)
- "All things work together for good to those who love God, to those who are the called according to His purpose." (Rom. 8:28 NKJV)
- "What great love the Father has lavished on us, that we should be called children of God! And that is what we are!" (1 John 3:1)

I knew these scriptures, sure. But though I'd been aware of them, though I'd incorporated them into the Bible studies I taught, I'd never experienced them—not really. The true experience of the Scriptures as love and life came only in the midnight of tragedy.

It wasn't supposed to be that way—not for me. But it was.

I listened again, and the same scriptures echoed. I heard the words, I suppose. But even more, I felt them pushing against all that denial, anger, and depression. I felt them working something like acceptance— acceptance of my disease, acceptance of my waning condition, acceptance that one day very soon, I would suffocate. And yet, this inkling of acceptance carried with it the richest, most nonsensical sense of faith, hope, love, and peace. I know now that this is the fruit of intimacy.

I let these promises soak past the skin, past the bone, into the heart.

It is God who will never leave. It is God who will send help. It is God who will work this all together for *his* good.

It is God.

It is God.

It has always been God.

I leaned into the richness of the promises, leaned into the love of the God who never leaves, always helps, and ever calls. I leaned into the new path and let go. Finally. It was the night I crucified the old John Paine, the capable, competent, self-sufficient, savvy, successful John Paine. It was the night I rose again, accepting and accepted, loved and now learning to love. Help had come, even in my darkest hour. I was sure of it.

It was Thanksgiving, months after my diagnosis and the midnight encounter with God. I'd become a student of Lou Gehrig's disease. I'd collected resources, spoken with doctor after doctor, and spent time with late-stage ALS patients. I was plotting out the path, considering my journey. All the materials confirmed it—there was no treatment that would stave off death, not really. But I wouldn't go down without a fight. I had resources, a war chest, and now was the time to open up the purse strings.

I took note of my holdings and compared them to my coming expenses. There would be wheelchairs and breathing apparatuses to purchase. There would be medical procedures and experimental treatments—should I consider stem cell treatment in South America or the ages-old naturopathic approaches in China? There would, of course, be hospice care to pay for, then a funeral.

I gathered my estate documents and reviewed the accounts. Now I wasn't searching for validation among the ones and zeros. Instead, I was counting the cost. I had learned to maximize the value of any company, had learned how to liquidate and wind one up. Now I was liquidating a life.

This is what getting your affairs in order looks like.

But as I leaned into acceptance—the acceptance of a fighter in the later rounds of a losing bout—I leaned into a new reality. I was in my late forties, and the prime of life was behind me. I considered this spasm of reality, and I felt the calming voice of Jesus somehow speaking in a quieter place, a place I was coming to know—*the heart*.

"Peace I leave with you, My peace I give to you. . . . Let not your heart be troubled, neither let it be afraid," he said (John 14:27 NKJV).

I considered those words in rhythm, as if on inhale and exhale.

Peace I leave with you.

My peace I give to you.

Let not your heart be troubled.

Neither let it be afraid.

Tears came; gratitude came too. There, in that moment of gratitude, emotions that had been buried for so many years came calling—sorrow, pain, self-doubt. They betrayed the artifice of perfection I'd worked so hard to project. I knew it then: I'd need to learn to come to grips with these emotions, to experience them, to understand them. I'd need to learn to release years of false beliefs to God. I had so much to learn about myself. Would I have enough time?

God reminded me again—*you are my child, loved more than you can know, and I am with you, always.* My doing, my striving, my success—none of it had brought this kind of closeness with God. But here in the dying, in the unbecoming, I was finding a mysterious wholeness.

Wholeness—how awkward to find it in the fractures of this once-perfect life.

PART III

The Intimacy

CHAPTER 11

The Undoing

The slow slide into ALS doesn't happen overnight, and I don't suppose the slide into intimacy is any different. ALS comes with its early warning signs—the twitching forearm, the loss of strength. Intimacy with God has its own spring shoots—an internal, connected presence that comforts in the midnight hour of sorrow, the sense of unconditional love wrapping you like a blanket. But ALS and intimacy are both progressive conditions.

Time passed as time does, and I found my symptoms creeping. My forearm twitched a little less, and as the fasciculations subsided, the strength drained. I considered the progression, how it had worked from my forearm down to my hand, up to my shoulder. I considered how it had spread down to my toes, up to my brow. I considered how it would seep inward, how it would work its atrophy into my diaphragm, how I'd find myself unable to breathe without a respirator, how my soul would stay tethered to this body only by the good grace of total life support.

And why keep my soul tethered to this failing body?

Why keep living with this constant, haunting fear?

"It is natural," the doctors say when handing down death sentences, "to be afraid." I know this because it was said to me. And what compelled the otherwise thoughtful doctor to say this? Was it meant to make me feel better about this blast crater in my stomach, the way I felt scooped hollow? Was it meant to put me at ease about the round-the-clock shock, the ringing in my ears? Maybe it was meant to normalize the nausea every time I considered those three letters—ALS. The fear that comes with contemplating total paralysis and death feels anything but natural, I wanted to tell them. But then again, how could they know? They'd treated hundreds of ALS patients, sure, but which of them had ever been on the business end of a death sentence? They were only doctors.

Fear, terminal diagnoses, intimacy—these are all things so easy to discuss in the abstract. The experience of them is something wholly other.

Weeks following my diagnosis, Margaret and I made our way back to the Neuromuscular Disorders clinic at UT Southwestern Medical Center, the same clinic where I'd been diagnosed. It was my first post-diagnosis appointment, and the wound was still fresh. I tried to put on my happiest face, but Margaret saw through it. We'd do this together, she said.

Together—it was a word I was coming to love.

We pulled up to the front of the clinic, where valet attendants waited to whisk the car away. We entered the front doors, stepped into the lobby, and made our way to the elevators. In the elevator, I felt my legs jelly up, felt my hands shaking. I reached for Margaret's hand, knowing she must be anxious too. We'd comfort each other, I thought. The elevator doors opened to a small room, and just across that waiting room, three attendants sat at a check-in counter. I stepped out first. Margaret followed.

I noticed the carpet; it was thin, institutional-grade stuff. The walls were cream-colored and barren. The attendants sat shoulder to shoulder, unsmiling. (The minutiae, the details of a room like that—why do they stick with you after so many years? Trauma sears things into memory, I think.)

I greeted the women at the desk, and one handed me a clipboard of papers to complete in triplicate. Papers—couldn't the medical community give terminal patients a break? Wasn't the universe of facts they needed to know limited to:

Name: *John Paine*

Symptoms: *ALS*

Occupation: *Winding up my affairs*

I took the clipboard and strode down a short hall to a more spacious waiting room. There, patients filled low-backed chairs lining the walls, and a television played an ALS informational program hosted by a smiling nurse. She was the only one smiling in the room. I chose a chair, and Margaret sat beside me as I scribbled answers and checked boxes. A name was called, and I looked up, scanning the room.

All these patients. All these victims. All these recipients of an unfair life. Here we all were, together in the dying.

A man in a wheelchair rolled toward the nurse at the open door, arms frozen in his lap, head strapped to the back of his chair. His wife pushed him silently.

They passed a woman in a rumpled black blouse who shuffled around the waiting room, unable to raise her feet above the carpet. Her husband held her elbow and forearm and shuffled next to her, eyes on her feet.

Another man sat in a wheelchair, unmoving, mouth agape, eyes darting from side to side. Drool traced a line from his mouth, down his chin, and pooled on a spit tray affixed to the arms of his chair.

I studied the room and noticed that the majority of patients had respirators of some kind, and the out-of-sync whirs created the sound of simultaneous pushing and pulling, sucking and snoring. That's when I noticed it: I was not breathing. Fear was suffocating me.

Breathe in; breathe out.

Find the rhythm.

Had I ever had to concentrate this hard to breathe?

There were muffled conversations around the room, garbled syllables falling from those who'd been robbed of muscle tone in their tongues and lips. The patients were, for the most part, in pajamas or sweatpants, clothes easy to slip in and out of. They wore long sleeves or light jackets, the outer garments of those whose circulatory systems can no longer pump warm blood to their extremities. A staleness hung in the waiting room. If there is a purgatory, this was it, the holding cell between life and eternity. And what of me? Would this be me in a few short months?

"Dear God . . . dear God . . . dear God, don't let this be me," I whispered, perhaps a bit too loud. Margaret looked at me, squeezed my hand. There was the fear again; it was choking my breath again. No one should receive such a potent foreshadowing of his own death. Was comfort in this kind of fear possible?

The bodies, the chairs, the faces of the caregivers—it was all catalyzing this fear. Hopelessness hung in the air, misery too. I could pray all I wanted, but this was my future—paralysis, lifelessness, maybe nothingness. And in that moment of terror, I heard death calling my name.

John Paine.

John Paine.

John Paine.

But it wasn't death at all. Instead, it was the nurse standing by the open door.

I walked toward the nurse, tall and strong, still able. How much longer until I had to shuffle my feet? How much longer until Margaret would need to wheel me through this door?

Behind the door, the nurse took me to a weigh station, and I removed my shoes and stepped on the scale. As she moved the sliders up and down the t-top, she told me that monitoring my weight would be a top priority.

"As ALS patients lose muscle tone, swallowing becomes difficult," she said. "You may notice that you're choking on liquids first, then solids. There's a temptation to stop eating when this happens, and we can effectively monitor whether you're getting enough calories by keeping an eye on your weight."

I considered it. Water, wine, bread, cake—would I lose everything I loved so much?

The nurse attempted a smile. "If you have trouble swallowing, don't stop eating. Just give us a call and we can teach you some swallowing techniques or consider putting you on a feeding tube. Okay?"

I counted the question as rhetorical and waited for her to jot my weight on the chart.

Margaret and I followed her into a tiny room, one just big enough for a table, a single guest chair, and a miniature bank of cabinets. On the cabinet desk were cotton balls, tongue depressors, and oversized metal safety pins. As the nurse turned to leave, Dr. Nations, the same doctor who'd diagnosed me with ALS, entered. This time she was smiling.

"Well, hey, John," she said in an almost singsong voice. Her expression was warm, inviting, kind. It was the first bit of warmth I'd felt since walking into the clinic.

We exchanged pleasantries before she asked me to take off my socks and shoes. While I stripped my feet naked, Dr. Nations reached for one of the oversized safety pins. She unhooked the needle from the top, took my foot in her left hand, and with her right, she traced the lightest line with the tip of that needle, starting at the tip of the heel and curving that line into a *J* along the pad of my foot. This was a reflex test, she said, before pulling a tuning fork from the pocket of her lab coat. She tapped it on her left hand, then placed it against the bone on my foot. The fork hummed, sending vibrations into my foot and up my leg, all in the key of E.

"Do you feel that?" she asked, and I told her I could.

"Does it hurt?"

"No."

"Good, good," she said, but I didn't know what was good about any of it. "ALS is a progressive degenerative disease of the motor neurons, but it won't diminish your response to stimuli. In fact, it may heighten it."

By *stimuli*, I supposed she meant pain.

She continued, telling me of the services available through the clinic and outlining a few potential treatments. We'd get a few baseline measurements of strength, she said, and then she called a nurse to take me into the testing room of the clinic.

"See you soon," the good doctor said with a smile, but I couldn't help but wonder whether that'd be true. Who knows how quickly ALS works its murder?

I followed a nurse to a strength-testing room, where I sat in front of a microelectronic scale hooked to a computer. Using cloth cuffs, she attached the scale to my foot and asked me to extend and retract it. She attached a different cuff to the machine, then tethered it to my leg and asked me to pull down. Next, it was attached to my hand, and I was asked to curl it, as if lifting a dumbbell. Using a series of different cuffs, she measured the strength in my back, then my torso, then my head and neck.

Look down.

Look up.

Turn your head to the left.

Good. Now to the right.

The machine spit measurements from an attached printer. These were the baselines, she told me, but I knew she meant these were my peak outputs. It was all downhill from here. The metrics from that printer would come to a series of zeros soon. Death would follow.

After completing the strength tests, the nurse took us back to the treatment room. There was a short and silent wait before a woman entered and introduced herself as a hospital social worker who specialized in serving the terminally ill. There were disability and Medicare benefits, which were immediately available, she said, before pausing. She conjured up an earnest expression, then asked, "Is anyone harming you? Are you receiving adequate care?"

I cast a sideways glance at Margaret, then looked back at the nurse, raising my eyebrows in a sort of *help me* expression. The social worker understood the joke and chuckled. Margaret slapped my arm and looked down without smiling. I straightened, told the social worker I was only teasing Margaret, and that, yes, I was receiving appropriate care. But then I asked, "Is abuse an issue for ALS patients?"

"Oh my," she said. "It is not common, but as some of our patients become more disabled, their family members, caregivers, or friends take advantage of them. Some report abuse and manipulation. Sometimes, their resources are stolen."

I felt the air sucked from the room as she gave her impromptu and anecdotal case study of ALS patient abuse. Some were shuffled from home to home, uncared for. Many were abandoned by their spouses. She recounted a fortune's worth of thievery. Estate documents turned up missing. She described the myriad of ways ALS subjects its hosts to humiliation, all with painful detail. These were the exceptions, she said, but they are the horror stories that haunt me, even still.

The social worker handed her card to me and left the room, concluding our visit. We hustled through the dreaded waiting room and escaped through the lobby's sliding double doors, handing our valet ticket to the attendant. We stood in that moment, holding hands, silent. Margaret stared at her feet. A minute passed. Then a moment.

What was a minute now, but the death of sixty able-bodied seconds? What was a moment but a series of tiny funerals?

Days passed, then months. Clinic visits came and went. My body began to show signs of change, of weakness, of incompetency. As my physical body deteriorated, something was happening below the surface. In my purgatory, I was learning to hear the voice of comfort, the voice of love that had spoken to me in my study. It was a voice that came to me in the early morning, and in the midnight hours too. As I listened, I woke into this epiphany: the real John Paine was not the man of accomplishment or competency; the real John Paine was the man beneath all those projections. God seemed most interested in the man beneath all those projections.

On occasion, fear came creeping in, and when it did, I listened with my inner ears. I'd listen and listen, and I'd recognize the familiar words God had first spoken to me in the study.

Peace I leave with you.

My peace I give to you.

Let not your heart be troubled.

Neither let it be afraid.

These were the earliest days of my disease, the days of fear, trauma, and pain. But without fear, without pain, I don't suppose I would have ever found my way to connection with God. I don't suppose I would have ever been able to see how powerless I was. This is where intimacy starts: an admission of our own powerlessness. I know that now.

ALS gave me a gift. It brought me to the edge of myself—my abilities, my confidences, my control—then pushed me over that edge, screaming. I didn't find the abyss over that edge, though; instead, I found the open arms of God waiting to welcome me into his life of unconditional love, validation, comfort, and peace. In my own powerlessness, I found myself welcomed by the Power of all powers.

That's grace.

Tonight, this theater of the able-bodied watches a crippled man share his story. I hope they know my life is not all funerals and hopelessness, though. Even last month, sitting in that clinic, I watched patients shuffle their feet, heard the rhythmic wheezing of ventilators. I saw rivulets of drool sliding from drooped jaws. But where was the suffocating fear? It'd long since been replaced with a tangible intimacy with a God who loves me as I am, not for what I can do. This is, maybe, the greatest mystery—God can use the most hellish of circumstances to bring us into a richer understanding and experience of his love.

Oh, the love of God.

It's now my turn to recline in the wheelchair, fire burning my bum. It's my turn to curse weeping bedsores and endure the itches you can't scratch. It's my turn, and yet, isn't there joy in all this?

Yes.

If I could stand and shout it in this theater, I would: there is a way into deeper intimacy, even if it starts in powerlessness, pain, and fear. The way, though, requires an undoing—an undoing of my notions of God, an undoing of my notions of self-sufficiency, and an undoing of false beliefs long nursed. It requires a sort of becoming, too—the becoming of a man of wholehearted connection with God, a trusting man, a man of vulnerability. This undoing and becoming was the work that brought me into intimate oneness with God. It's what brought me into wholeness.

"Let them learn to be one with you," I whisper in prayer, "even as I learned to be one with you."

The images continue to flicker across the screen. Minutes turn to moments. What is a minute but being sixty seconds closer to my final moment? What is the final moment but the transition into the hope of eternity with God? This is the hope of eternity: all things past somehow being redeemed, even this hell.

CHAPTER 12

Cosmonauts and Snake Venom

I was knee-deep in the second year of my diagnosis when I stumbled across a promising article in the local newspaper. A neurologist at the University of Southern California was researching the effects of common chemical sprays containing neurotoxins on the brain, sprays such as commercial pesticides and household roach sprays. He theorized that these chemicals—chemicals that make their way into every modern American home—might have a causal connection to neurological disorders such as ALS, and he thought he might have discovered a treatment. I considered his hypothesis, wondered if government health agencies would approve these sprays for sale if they were really that dangerous. And if it were true, wouldn't ALS be more prevalent? Wouldn't it affect more than thirty thousand Americans? And how could you cure long-term exposure to these chemicals with just a few years of treatments? How could anyone grow new brain cells?

I dug deeper and read as much of the good doctor's research as I could. I discovered that his hypothesis was based on literature he'd discovered in reviewing the Russian cosmonaut program of the 1960s and 1970s. After spending time in space, cosmonauts were given an inhalant meant to counteract radiation poisoning, he said. This inhalant traversed the blood-brain barrier—a thin membrane designed to keep blood from flowing directly over the brain tissue. By traversing the BBB, as the barrier is sometimes called, the inhalant delivered certain medicine directly to the brain tissue, and though researchers didn't understand quite why, it appeared that this inhalant did more than cure radiation poisoning. The research suggested that the inhalant counteracted neurotoxin poisoning and stimulated neural healing. It was said that cosmonauts had an uncommonly low incidence of neurological disorders, including ALS. The magic was in the inhalant, the doctor had postulated, and he'd assembled a study to prove his theory.

It seemed like so much science fiction or an exercise in communist book-cooking, but what if his theory were correct? It was a nagging thought.

As a steeled man of business, I was wary of experimental cures and magic bullets. Still, there was something about the story I found fascinating, almost mysterious. And so, on little more than a few newspaper clippings, a hunch, and a nostalgic fascination for the space race of my childhood, I picked up the phone and dialed the neurologist's office in Los Angeles. The receptionist answered, and I told her my story, told her I had the means to make it to the research facility, and asked whether the doctor might be willing to include me in his study. They were taking volunteers, she said, but there were strict requirements for the program. I'd need to stay for two weeks and agree to two-week follow-up visits every few months for more testing. While in the program, I could only eat certain kinds of fish and specific vegetables.

"Still interested?" she asked.

"What do I have to lose?" I asked.

"On the upside, you and your wife will have evenings all to yourself in beautiful Southern California."

I smiled. With ALS, you learn to make the most of any advantage, fleeting as they are.

Weeks later, we arrived at our temporary home in San Clemente, California, just thirty minutes from the testing facility. I'd begun experiencing trouble walking, my feet feeling as if they were weighted with lead. Knowing Margaret would want to spend the evenings walking together on the beach, I made arrangements. Before purchasing our tickets, I'd called ahead to make sure the airline could check my Segway—a personal, self-balancing scooter sort of contraption I'd purchased in anticipation that I'd soon need it. The details had been sorted (airlines will check any disability assistive device at no extra charge, whether a wheelchair, walker, shower chair, ventilator, or Segway), and there we were—Margaret, me, and my Segway—with two weeks of evenings to kill.

The first few days of tests passed with whirlwind intensity, but the evenings were all peace. Before sunset, we made our way to the pier, me rolling and Margaret strolling. Some evenings we found ourselves dining at a white tablecloth restaurant overlooking the ocean, while on others, we bought fresh fish from the market to grill at the condo. We laughed together, held hands across every table. We were finding a sort of grace in this tragedy of inevitability, a fresh joy in being together, even in my pain. Why? Who could say, other than God was changing my heart. Powerlessness was my new reality, and in that, so many of our old hang-ups seemed petty and insignificant. I needed Margaret more than ever, and why should I spend it controlling, manipulating, or criticizing her? Why should she soak in negativity? I was accepting her as she was, even though I couldn't have put it into words just yet. She was accepting me, too, disability and all. We were on the mend.

A week passed, and the Pacific coast kept working its magic into us. It felt like a new season of closeness, of love, and the evening sunsets colored everything a shade of rose. These were the first inklings that Margaret and I were cultivating the kind of intimacy I'd wanted for so many years, an intimacy that'd been building since my first visit to Al-Anon. We'd fallen back into a deep, fierce love, even deeper and fiercer than before. But what did it mean to sense the love of God this tangibly? Was such a thing possible?

Our time in California was drawing to a close, and Margaret and I made our way to the beach for one of our last evening walks. The gulls cried and sandpipers poked their straw-like beaks into the shallows. The palms blew in the wind, their fronds swishing, and as I motored forward, I closed my eyes to fix that moment in my memory. I felt the wind against my cheeks. I heard the squeals of children playing on the edge of the surf, the patter of runners' feet passing on my left and right. There was the world, all active and pleasant, but where was God in it? Was he here, even with all of us? Was his love soaking all of us?

Teach me about your love, I prayed. It was a simple, earnest request, and I don't suppose I expected such an immediate answer. Eyes still closed, an image came, a vision. There I was, standing on the beach, a river passing in front of me and flowing out toward the ocean. I turned and traced the river back to its source. Behind me, perhaps fifty yards, was a sandstone wall near the edge of the beach. A trickle of water cut through its center, then ran down to its base. From the bottom of the rock wall, the small stream ran onto the beach and carved a path down, growing in size until it was a full-fledged river just in front of me. It kept growing, kept swelling, until it consumed the beach, until

I was in the middle of it, somehow. The river pushed strong into the ocean, carrying silt past me and into the depths. It pushed past the islands on the horizon, even over the continental shelf. This river filled the ocean, I thought, and all of it started with a trickle cutting through a stony wall.

I saw all of this in a split second, almost as if in a memory, and in that same split second, I felt the comfort and peace I'd first come to know in my office. That's when the whisper came, deep in my heart.

This is what my love is like—breaking through rock and always growing, always spreading out in front of my people, always sweeping them up in it, always filling the earth. It is an unfathomable, unmeasurable, incomprehensible, complete, and unconditional love.

This love, did I know it really? I considered that river and felt its force. I'd been a follower of Christ for decades, so why had I never understood the penetrating, sweeping, powerful fullness of God's love? Why had I never experienced this kind of infinite wholeness? Why did I think God's love was contingent on my hard work, my ability to build a canal to divert a portion of it my way? Why was it so difficult to accept, to understand the breadth and depth of this unconditional love?

The questions were rhetorical, but the answer was not.

My father.

I reached into my memory, remembered his disapproving gaze, the way his approval was always conditioned on performance, on achievement, on success. I remember believing that if I could just measure up, then I'd receive his love and acceptance. His love was limited, finite, conditioned. He did the best he knew how, I suppose, but his best had wounded me. And somehow, I'd conflated my natural father with the Father of the supernatural.

Father, father, father—what did it mean to have a loving father?

That's when the scriptures came, but they came in a new language. They came like messages meant just for me.

You are my adopted child.

I sensed the crack in my stony heart, felt a trickle of love.

You are my son.

This stream of love pooled, began to fill me.

I am love. Know and rely on the love I have for you.

Here was the river, picking up the sediment of my pain, the silt of all my wasted efforts to matter.

Know my love, my unending, immeasurable love without conditions. I love because I am love, and my love is bigger than you can understand. My love will fill you with my fullness, just as you are, regardless of your performance, even in your emptiness.

I was now in the ocean of his love, and for the first time in so many years, I could feel. There was freedom, gratitude, joy, even sorrow for the years lost—I felt it all. More than anything, though, I felt wholly known, fully accepted, and loved without any requirement to measure up. I might not ever earn the success I'd chased for so many years in so many areas of my life, but in this love, I realized the gospel truth—I didn't need to. This love—there was nothing to do but receive it just as it was, just as it was receiving me.

I felt Margaret's hand touch my arm.

"John?"

I turned to her, smiling.

"Are you okay?"

"Yes," I said. "I couldn't be better."

It was my first taste of oneness with God's love, and I wondered— was this the way Jesus felt as he walked the earth? Yes, I supposed. The mystery of Christ must be this: Jesus knew, understood, and was ever incorporated into the great ocean of God's love. He knew this in his innermost parts, in his inner man, and he wanted us to know this love too. This must be another facet of salvation.

———— ⁂ ————

I found the spring of real living in Los Angeles, but not the well of physical healing. After enduring months of experimental treatments with the cosmonaut inhalant, I came up dry. There was no magic bullet there, nothing that might arrest the progress of my disease. I suppose life is full of give-and-take propositions, and giving my time and money to chase a pipe dream was worth the experience of true love.

Having reached a dead end in California, I resumed my search for healing. Organized as I was—some might call it hypervigilant—I'd constructed a matrix of medical opportunity, a spreadsheet showing potential treatments, their reported likelihood of success, and whether the results were sustainable past six months. The opportunity at USC now marked off the list, I moved to the next potential treatment. Stem cell transplants.

I'd discovered it while watching the evening news. The correspondent stood in the heart of Beijing, bundled against the cold outside a research lab. There was a doctor, he said, who claimed miraculous results by injecting stem cells directly into the brains of ALS patients. The footage was mesmerizing: patients were wheeled into the lab, unable to move, and mere hours later, those same patients walked out. A man who was unable to talk before treatment, walked out of the clinic and offered a full interview to the correspondent. If these results could be replicated in even a small sample of ALS patients, the treatment was promising.

I tracked down the lab, called, and paid for a spot on the waiting list. I bought a ticket to China for Margaret and me and went shopping for a heavy coat (the weather in Beijing was colder than a well digger's heinie, a traveling friend said). I pushed ahead, but as I researched more, I realized just how experimental the treatments were. I discovered the doctors introduced the stem cell cultures into the brain by drilling a hole through the skull. It was their theory that the cultures could take root in the brain and create new neural pathways, reversing the symptoms of ALS. And though the newsreels and articles showed tremendous results, the invasive nature of the procedure gave me great pause.

I approached the nurses at the ALS clinic, asked them whether they knew anyone who'd undergone the treatment. They did, they said, but due to privacy concerns they couldn't give me the names.

"Can you share my name with any of those patients? Would you ask them to give me a call?" I asked. Helpful as they were, hope giving as they were, they agreed, and within days, I received a phone call from a patient who'd made the trip to China. The results were incredible, she said, but only for three days. After that, her symptoms came leaking back. For twenty thousand dollars and no small amount of travel expenses, she'd bought the nostalgia of the days before ALS. But moving from nostalgia back into the reality of the disease was a sort of torture.

"It's not sustainable," she said. "It's snake venom."

Snake venom—a reference to the cobra venom injections that were all the hope among ALS patients a few years before. Urban legend had it that an ALS patient bitten by a cobra in the Far East had barely escaped with his life, but when he woke in the hospital, his symptoms were gone. Vanished. A miracle. Doctors tried for years to reproduce the results (some said), with no success. It was a fluke. Maybe it was all a myth. Who can say?

I spoke to a few others who'd made the trek to China, and their reports were the same. They sought hope, had paid a high price for it. But in each case, the results were similar. Three days, six days, less than a month—every patient suffered the same outcome. Snake venom. And this is what happens in the world of terminal illness: healers peddle half-truths, search for half-cocked cures, and they grow rich doing it. All the while we, the patients, continue down the road to suffocation. There is no end to the opportunism of men. There is no shortage of snake oil salesmen or snake venom peddlers.

There are so many treatments, so many clinics or experiments that offer hope to ALS patients, but this hope is as shifty as Pacific sand. Experimental labs, holistic nutritionists, ancient folk medicine, Eastern remedies, they all offer pipe dream after pipe dream. Hope sells. Potential sells. And what's the buyer left with? A lighter wallet and still-certain death sentence.

⸺✕⸺

I'm on the screen again, supersized and speaking with the camera about the early days of my diagnosis. "It's frightening to think about the future, because no one gets better."

No one gets better. Not the cosmonauts. Not the snake bitten. Not the stem cell recipients. Not me. These are the facts of ALS; these are the facts of life and death.

CHAPTER 13

Sneaky Theologies

There are sneaky theologies that take root in the lives of all men, and I was no exception. My own sneaky theologies took root somewhere past conscious belief and motivated me in ways that were almost involuntary. And though God had shown me the truth of his unwieldy, unconditional, unfathomable love, I still wondered: Could he give me something more? Would he bless me with some miracle of healing?

The medical arts were proving no match for the onset of my symptoms, and as my legs grew heavier, as my breath became shorter, as I began to lose the use of my left hand, some friends, well-intentioned family members, and an intermeddler or two took notice. They came to my office, called me, sent me emails. Time after time, they suggested a spiritual solution. Healing was available, they said, so long as I did my part.

"Confess your sins," they said, quoting the scripture in James, "so that you may be healed" (5:16). This, of course, they took to mean physical healing. They co-opted the words of Christ, too, telling me that if I had faith, Jesus would answer my cries for healing. Some asked whether I'd made any secret agreements with the devil, agreements that bound me up in illness (whatever that meant). Others asked whether there were generational sins that might explain my sickness.

Solutions, solutions, solutions—everyone had the formula for a solution-oriented outcome, and that outcome was ever and always complete physical healing. But all these formulas—aren't they convenient when you're not the one suffocating to death?

It is true—some of these more charismatic theologies didn't square with my earlier, more conservative belief system. Still, what if God really wanted to heal me? I wanted to believe. Would I be so stubborn as to give up on that possibility?

Lord, help my unbelief.

A dear friend, a pastor from a church in the suburbs, came to my office with a word, he said. There was a world-renowned healer from California visiting a local church for a healing revival. Would I come? he asked. With nothing to lose, I agreed.

Nights later, I sat in the gut of a hollowed-out warehouse that had been converted into a church. A band whipped the crowd into a worshipful lather with ethereal, almost hypnotic music, and the singers raised songs of deliverance. These were not the hymns of my Presbyterian youth or my Baptist young adulthood. These were more akin to the songs of the Bible church I attended in those days, impromptu songs of worship. Band members and congregants alike closed their eyes and swayed. One cried. Another smiled as if in ecstasy. Hands were raised—a near impossibility for me, arms heavy with ALS as they were.

After what seemed like the better part of an hour, the band tapered and began playing the type of mood music you might hear in the elevator of a classy high-rise. That's when the healer took the stage.

He was measured in his words and manner, and his voice was pure velvet. In that smooth baritone, he asked how God could refuse to heal someone when he'd already bought their healing on the cross. "And by his stripes, you *are* healed," he said, quoting the prophet Isaiah, then iterated that this healing was not just spiritual, but physical.

"He's purchased your complete healing, spiritual and physical. So, what's the problem?" I felt the weight of the question. "Maybe the problem isn't with God; maybe the problem is your inability to receive God's healing."

There it was. The accusation. And yet, didn't this somehow seem right?

He went on to describe those he'd seen healed. The cook in Lincoln, healed of a severe burn. The crosswalk guard in Los Angeles whose leg grew two inches, who now walked without a limp. "I've seen these things," he said, "and do you know the common denominator? Faith." On and on he went, sharing stories so that our faith might grow, he said. Faith, faith, faith—it's all about faith.

"There is no doubt: it is God's will for everyone to be healed." There was not a hint of doubt in his voice. "He wants to bring perfection to imperfection. Do you believe?"

He opened the aisles, and near the front as I was, I labored my way to the head of the forming line. A few dozen folks beat me to the front and were standing in the well of the sanctuary between the stage and the first row. I waited, watched as these people who'd made it to the stirring waters of healing waited for their miracles. The healer prayed en masse over the lot of us, sloshing the blood of Jesus over our illnesses. He then went from person to person in the well of the sanctuary, putting his hand on each of their foreheads. As he prayed, the band resumed their songs of spontaneous worship, and I waited, body aching, heavy as a millstone.

Minutes passed. Then more minutes. Just before the weight of my body threatened to push me to the floor, the healer stood eye to eye with me. He noted the curling fingers on my left hand, my trembling legs, and he asked me what was wrong. I spoke those three letters—ALS—and told him this was a disease that would paralyze me, tear me limb from limb, then suffocate me. He looked in my eyes, face too earnest for empathy, and he chided, "You really can't believe that. You can't identify with your disease."

Identify with my disease? Did it really matter? Hadn't ALS picked me out of the billions of people in the world? Hadn't it identified me? I wanted to tell him I didn't choose the disease, that I hadn't wrapped my identity up in it. I didn't believe I *was* ALS, but that I was just the unlucky fella who'd contracted it. I wanted to speak, but I was not the authority. He was. And he didn't give me the space of a response.

His prayer was as earnest as his face and just as empathetic. He declared that my healing was sealed in the heavens, that it'd already taken place. He thanked Jesus for the work, In-Jesus'-Name-Amened, then looked back into my eyes.

"Keep believing," he said. "This is your only job. Not all healing is immediate; you must continue to receive it by faith. If you have full faith, you'll see the miracle of healing in your body over time. It is God's will that you be completely, totally, utterly healed."

With that, he moved to the next short-order cook with a burn, the next crosswalk guard with a limp, the next cancer patient or common cold sufferer, the next whatever. Promises, promises—he made them to everyone. But these were contingent promises. God would heal everyone who had faith. Only believe, he said to us all.

As I returned to my seat, a man nudged me. I looked to my right, saw the brass collection plate. Unable to raise my hands, unable to take the plate, unable to even reach my wallet, I looked up at him, blinking. Maybe it was part of the deal, I guessed. Maybe every miracle comes with a collection.

———— ✕ ————

More snake venom. More opportunism. There's money to be made in the healing arts, medical, spiritual, or otherwise. But still, didn't I believe healing was possible? Hadn't Jesus healed Peter's mother? Didn't he raise Lazarus? Wasn't Christ the healer of those who served him? Yes, yes, yes, yes—I believed all these things. So, why should I give up after one negative experience? The truth is, I believed God blessed his people with healing.

Perhaps it was the messenger and not the medium, I thought. Maybe the faith healer's art wasn't meant for me or anyone else that night. (To the best of my knowledge, not a single person walked out of that warehouse healed.) But I knew another man, a man I loved and trusted, and I'd seen the healing power of God working through him.

I'd first met Apostle Chipaya, a Zambian pastor, the year of my diagnosis. He'd been brought to my office by a close friend who said the diminutive but stocky man of God might hold the answer to my healing. I was skeptical at first, of course, but as he walked into my office, I noted his palpable warmth, his infectious smile. We prayed for more than two hours on that first meeting, and as he prayed, I felt the richest sense of God's presence. Apostle Chipaya was aware of God's ability to heal, but he made no promises and didn't tie anything to my faith or lack of it. And it was in that first meeting that I knew it—Apostle Chipaya and I would become close friends.

Over the next three years, Apostle Chipaya returned to the States every six months or so, and he came to my office each time. On each visit, he stayed a bit longer, spending most of that time in prayer with me. He begged God for my healing but watched as three years' worth of unanswered prayers left ALS to ravage my body. It was on the last of these visits that he asked me a question in his broken British accent.

"What do sick Christians do in America when they need healing?"

"We visit the doctor."

"Of course," he said, then paused for effect. "I suppose this is because you have so many talented doctors. In Zambia we go straight to God. He's all so many of us have. Maybe that's why I see more healings in my home country."

This was neither an accusation nor an assertion. It was a working hypothesis.

"Would you like to visit me in Zambia?" he asked. "Maybe I could ask the elders at my church to pray for you?"

He paused, gave space for his words to stick. Then, he mustered more force. "John, come to Africa."

Desperate as I was, curious as I was, adventuresome as I was, I agreed. I'd always wanted to see Africa, but I had hoped it'd be for business or pleasure. The days of business and pleasure trips were running thin, though; death was the poacher, hunting me. If I was to see Africa it'd be for healing, and resigned to this fact I purchased two tickets. A month later, my eldest son, John, and I were on a flight across the Atlantic.

It was a sixty-degree morning in Lusaka, Zambia. We were met on the tarmac by customs agents and escorted to a VIP lounge in the airport. In the lounge, Apostle Chipaya thundered his welcome as we entered the room. We exchanged hugs, and he said we'd need to hurry to his home. People were waiting, he said. There'd be plenty of time to see the sights, the exotic wildlife, and Victoria Falls, but first, we'd start with a prayer meeting.

At his home, we were greeted by Apostle Chipaya's wife, Emily, and the elders of his church, together with their wives. After lunch and a time of rest, we gathered in his living room and turned to prayer. That house full of people prayed, and prayed, and prayed. They asked me whether I needed to confess sins, or whether there was any unforgiveness blocking my healing. They explored certain "spiritual blocks to healing" (whatever those were) and the potential that spiritual warfare was causing my disease. They asked questions about my family background, asked whether there might be any family curses that had caused me to contract ALS. So many of the questions were the same as those asked in the States, but the tone was different, somehow purer. We prayed for more than three hours that first night; little did I know, we were just getting started.

The next three days followed a consistent schedule: sightseeing in the morning, rest in the afternoon, prayer in the evening. Between meetings, I met men who'd been healed from various maladies—withered hands, crippled legs, blindness, AIDS. I heard the stories, and yet each of them reminded me that God does not always heal—an honest recognition in light of the many illnesses and maladies plaguing the Zambian people. Still, I trusted that God could do a miracle for me among this people of fierce belief. And so, we dedicated ourselves to prayer and exploration in the evenings, hoping for some sort of breakthrough. I exercised every ounce of faith I had, envisioned myself moving, even tried to wiggle my fingers. I saw myself running, even tried to pick my legs higher off the ground. But after twenty hours of prayer, nothing had changed. My body was still as heavy as a sack of wet concrete. I was still dying.

Somewhere over the Atlantic, I jotted notes in a journal with my still-working right hand. There are so many camps to this healing thing, I wrote. Most Christians would say God can still heal—if he wants to, that is—but a smaller subset would say it's God's will that *all* should be healed. Doesn't this theology imply that those who aren't healed, don't have a faith that measures up? Doesn't it produce so much guilt, shame, and doubt? Doesn't it reinforce the idea that we can somehow conjure God's favor, God's blessing, God's love?

God had taught me that his love was not conditioned on my works, my abilities, the sum of my faith. And I knew it was the same with his healing. So why was I so disappointed?

I looked up from my journal, searched my thoughts. My eyes blurred, and the fire of sorrow rose in my throat.

Oh God, I want your healing.

Oh God, I know you can heal me.

Oh God, I would tell everyone of your miracle.

Oh God, haven't I done enough for you?

There it was. That sneaky bootstraps theology came bubbling up to the surface—God should bless me because of the work I'd done for him. Its roots stretched deep, even into my beliefs about healing. Even as I was learning about the unmerited, unconditional love of God, I was still trying to earn my own miracle. It turns out, this is not God's way.

I turned to prayer, confessed it all.

I don't want this paralysis.

I don't want nerve pain.

I don't want to suffocate.

I don't want to die.

I don't want to drink from ALS's cup.

Tears splashed on the page, mingled with the fresh ink, and created spreading globs with blue-black ganglion. One looked like a brain; another resembled a cloud. Grief built, washed over me in fresh waves, and washed over the page too. That's when the painful reality set in. I would not be healed this side of heaven.

In the quietness of my seat, my son sleeping to my left and a large Zambian man sleeping to my right, I prayed through all those tears. "I thought this life would be more fair," I tried to choke out, but no sooner had the words gathered in my mouth than I heard the echo of a silent response.

I understand, John.

I knew this voice at once; it was the voice of Christ.

I imagined his life, how it all culminated in the pain of being tacked to a crossbeam. He was paralyzed in the position of crucifixion, unable to lift his legs or lower his arms. He endured searing pain, the nerves shot through by nails, thorns, the tails of a whip. As his final hours came to a close, the weight of his torso crushed down on his lungs, suffocating him. This Christ—couldn't he understand my ALS?

I sat in the moment, united with Christ in his pain. God made man and then stepped into his own creation in the person of Jesus. And yet, not everything went his way. He was a man of healing, yes. But though he brought healing to others, though he prayed that the cup of pain might pass from him, he still endured the ultimate suffering. He took up the cross meant for him, and by way of that cross, he lived into the will of his Father.

Was it possible that God's will for my life required this cross of ALS? Was it possible that he wanted to shape me into the image of Christ? Was it possible that there was some purpose in this pain, in my disability? Was God more committed to internal healing than external? Was it possible that I should conform to his will rather than my own?

The question hung, but not too long. I knew the answer, and I heard it in the quiet.

My grace is sufficient; my power is made perfect in your weakness.

A transformation was underway, a revolution in my way of being. God was healing me where it mattered the most. It was not God's desire that all should be healed of every malady, and there was no way to earn this sort of miraculous gift any more than there is a way to earn his love. If there were, wouldn't Christ have been able to pray the cup of his own pain away? Of all the people who'd ever lived, wasn't he righteous and faith-full enough?

Through the lens of Christ's passion, it became clear—God's intimacy isn't best expressed by providing his people with a pain-free existence. Intimacy is best expressed by meeting us in the pain and becoming the comfort we need in the moment, even when we feel abandoned. In that realization, that moment, a new comfort washed over me.

Christ once quoted the words of Isaiah, said he came to bind up the brokenhearted, and brokenhearted as I was, I felt his comfort dressing my wounds. Yes—this was comfort, and in that comfort, I sensed the whisper I'd grown so accustomed to hearing.

I am with you, always.

I will never leave you.

I love you more than you can ever know.

There is even deeper healing coming.

I share this theater with people of sneaky theologies. Do they wonder whether my sickness is some divine punishment, whether their own sicknesses are? Do some of them figure the demons are winning? Do they judge my faith inadequate for divine healing? Can anyone really believe that it requires a better faith to be healed than to be saved? I don't know, and to be frank, I don't suppose I care.

I've heard the stories of healing, and I believe many of them. I know the God who took the form of Christ himself can reach down and heal any malady. He can, yes, but does he always? No. Here's the platinum lining, though: the God of intimacy brings his comfort to the inner place, to the broken heart. In that comfort, he brings healing and transformation. He holds me even when I can't see it or feel it. Without suffering, without pain, without the hell of this chair, I'd have never discovered this comfort, this healing, this transformation. I'd have never discovered intimacy with him. I wouldn't trade that for anything.

The pain is churning now, and I consider all those unanswered prayers for healing. A blue shot of electricity radiates from my feet into my shins, up my thighs and into my bottom. It is a pulsing current. I could wallow in the "why" questions, even now, but what good would that do? The "why" questions only highlight the pain, only prolong it. Pain is the reality of my life, but even in this pain, I know there's a God of comfort. I know because he's here now, holding me.

I close my eyes, sink into his presence. I feel him like a daddy. I hear his voice, tender as it was all those years ago.

Do not fear, for I am with you. I will uphold you with my right hand. Just a little longer, John. My grace is sufficient for you, and my power is made perfect in your weakness.

The pain persists, but this comfort, this care, this hope, is a total eclipse. The bright burning dulls, fades to black, and I am left in this theater with my God. It is the cool of my life's evening, and here we are, together. How grand.

CHAPTER 14

Real Paine

I smile as I look at the screen. My friend Gary Wood is there, and he outs the truth of my life.

"Like many men, John and I confessed to each other that one of the difficulties in our Christian life was that of control," he said. "Males typically want to be in control all the time, and John was no different in that. He'd tell you that. He was a control freak. The thing that John said he learned out of this was to give that up."

I wish it had been that simple. I wish I would have received my diagnosis and my control complexes would have sloughed off like dead skin. But how do any of our bad habits die without being exposed, without being confessed, without being killed?

Control, control, control—yes, I was a control freak. But what was the thing behind it?

For so long the noise drove me. The phone calls, voice messages, business meetings—these were all markers of my success, indications that I was in demand. Now a different noise had set in—the phone calls to remind me of appointments, the progress reports, the meetings with doctors. Noise, a thing I'd become so accustomed to for most of my life, now seemed like such a distraction. With all this noise, was it possible to practice the presence of God?

I told Margaret that the noise had grown too loud, that the appointments, calls from friends, pop-in visits from ministers, not to mention my continuing business obligations, were just too much. I needed dedicated quiet space. I needed time to prepare for the coming losses. I wanted dedicated time to search the Scriptures, to read, to sit and listen for the voice of God.

Margaret looked at me, head cocked. "Are you okay?" she asked, knowing I wasn't prone to solitude or quiet. I'd been a man of activity, one who'd loved noise for so long, especially if that noise centered around my accomplishments. This request didn't jibe with the old John Paine.

"This feels like a calling," I said. "I don't know how else to put it." I paused, gathered my thoughts. "But it can't just be something for me. I want you to come too. I want you to be in this with me."

She searched my face then took my dead left hand. "Okay," she said. "Let's make it happen."

I put out feelers, began looking for a quiet backcountry retreat. There were requirements: a landline, limited access to television, no cell phone reception, and limited access to the internet. I scoured the web and gathered real estate magazines from Colorado that specialized in backcountry properties. I began to reach out to my network of friends, too, and one of them knew just the place. My friend and business colleague,

A. C. Musgraves, said he'd spoken with a couple of his friends who owned a place in Colorado. Don and Deyon Stephens were the founders of Mercy Ships, a nonprofit organization that converted cruise ships into floating hospitals that stopped in impoverished ports of call to provide services to the poor. They owned a rustic home deep in the Cimarron Mountain Range, A. C. said, and after hearing our story, they'd offered to let us stay there for a month that summer.

"You'll have the property to yourself for a month," he said. "Interested?"

He didn't have to ask twice.

It was the beginning of August, those sweltering days when the Texas heat hard-boils you. The appointed day for our escape had come, and so, SUV loaded, we cut a line up Highway 287. We slid through the overheated Texas Panhandle and across barren northeast New Mexico landscape, where short grasses, dry as matchsticks, stuck up in patches from the russet dirt. Through those plains we made our way into the heart of the Rockies, into craggy passes and patchwork evergreen forests. We climbed the pass at Monarch, the valley visible thousands of feet below the highway. We dropped down into Gunnison, drove past the reservoir, and fell into the cradling arms of the Cimarron Mountain Range.

A gravel road peeled off to the left, and the navigation system told us this was our turn. Across the road, a produce truck was parked, its bed loaded with produce. A sign read "COLORADO FRESH." Local produce, in such an arid climate? A man, tan as leather, stood by the back of the truck and smiled, waving as we turned south and began to climb into the belly of the mountains.

It was a slow and steady climb up the gravel road, and as we made our way deeper into the interior, I noticed the cattle ranches dotting the valley. We made a cutback and found ourselves on a bridge cutting through an aspen grove, the narrow slit of a river running below. Another cutback, and we found ourselves on the gentle slope of a mountainside, an irrigation canal running parallel to the road. I'd later learn that this was the canal that carried snowmelt down to the valley, down to the farmers in Palisades, who grew the sweetest peaches.

I looked at my phone, which had no reception now, and that's when the quiet settled in. I'd never been away from the obligations and responsibilities of my life for a month. I'd never allowed myself this kind of reprieve. I'd always lived with an eye on the future, striving into the next deal, the next church obligation, even the next family vacation itinerary. But now, armed with the certainty of God's love and resting in the certainty of my own death, life looked so much different. The future—it was an uncertain thing, so full of half-truths. The present was all I had, and I intended to live into it.

This present moment.

This present mountain.

This present beauty.

This present Margaret.

We pulled up to the cabin as the sun set over the far range in a warm glow. Below the cabin, I heard the river running, envisioned fly fishermen pushing their lines through the air, splaying them across the water, waiting for the rising trout.

The Stephenses left us the keys to a four-wheeler and maps to all the best trails, the more secluded overlooks, the hidden lakes and waterfalls, and the most majestic passes. In the mornings, we'd rise slowly and sit outside in the shadows of those mountains, drinking coffee and reading. After lunch, we'd climb on the four-wheeler, Margaret in the front and me with my arms around her waist, grasping my now-dead left hand with my right. We made our way into the ragged mountains, found quiet places for silence and prayer. Near the end of the first week, we followed the map and made the one-hour jaunt to West Fork, the place the Stephenses indicated was their favorite. There, I found the best perch, a place to set up my camping chair in the shadows of the crags knifing into the low-slung clouds.

In the silence, I could feel it. Oh, the love of God. The voice of that love—I could even hear it.

I am Love.

I looked across the valley, saw the grazing deer.

I am with you always.

To my left a marmot scurried under a log, squeaking.

Find rest in my love.

A coyote darted into an aspen grove, hunting.

After a few hours of sitting in the glory of the Cimarrons, Margaret and I returned to the house for the evening. On that bumpy ride back, I sensed there was something I needed to learn, something God wanted to work into me for the coming years of pain and paralysis. What was it?

We settled deeper into the mountain rhythm in the days that followed, found ourselves spending hours sipping coffee in the quiet, or sharing longer meals, or sleeping well past sunrise. We spent our afternoons exploring the backcountry, hunting for the presence of God in the aspen groves, river runs, or shadows of those craggy peaks. He was easier to find in those mountains; in fact, he was everywhere I looked. My heart was awakening to his presence all around me.

The days were slow, but the weeks passed faster than I imagined they could. This month of time, what I considered to be such a large expanse of time, was drawing to a close. But this month had been such an experience of the presence of God, and I could feel it even now—my heart was awakening.

We decided to make the most of it, and on one of those last days, Margaret strapped camping chairs to the four-wheeler. We mounted up and made the longer haul back out to West Fork. I'd been learning to rest in this love of God, but on that day, I came with an agenda.

I'd always been so good with agendas.

In the weeks before we left for Colorado, a question plagued me: *What validates me?* The question came at the most inopportune times. I'd made a career of brushing off the questions of the soul, though, and was a professional at ditching things I didn't want to consider. And yet, I couldn't ditch this question. When I was in the car, looking at the map, there it was. Just before drifting to sleep, there it was. The question nagged and nagged, and so, coming into the quiet of the Cimarron Range, I decided to wrestle down an answer.

We reached West Fork, and Margaret set up my camping chair. I shuffled to it, Margaret holding my arm, and I was careful not to trip on the rocks and limbs on the path. I sat down, took in the midmorning view, and waited for the question to come. This time, though, it came with a more personal flair.

What validates you, John?

He'd asked me by name, and I didn't hesitate.

"You, Lord. You know it's you."

There was a long pause, and a deep discomfort set in.

Everything validates you but me, John.

Could it be that he was speaking to the wrong John Paine? Hadn't I always done my best to serve God? And in this season of disease—this crippling, unfair disease—hadn't I given in to his plan and purpose? Hadn't I accepted the cup of my suffering?

Mind hijacked, racing to defend myself, the memory of all those cards falling like leaves in my study came dancing back. I thought I had already dealt with this question. Hadn't I?

Consider your businesses. Consider the ones that failed. How'd that make you feel?

Was I hearing things? If I was, how could it ring so true?

"I felt like I lost control; I felt like a failure."

You felt like a failure because of a lost business, John?

The question pierced, but that piercing brought such clarity. The businesses, the positions, the bank accounts, the drive to win, to structure, to succeed, to control every outcome—I'd used all of it to prove I was worthy of respect, if not love. Through business, I could establish worth—both self- and net. What was this if not an attempt to substantiate myself in the eyes of so many men around me? What was this if not an attempt to find validation? And desperate for that validation, I projected a certain image, a false one: I was the most capable of all; I existed above failure. I hid behind storied versions of my business failures so colleagues and friends wouldn't think less of me. I wore masks, created facades. Failure and the admission of it was not possible, because failure spoke to the deepest wound—I'd never be enough. The narratives designed to gain validation—what were they but attempts to keep fear, failure, or pain at arm's length?

I would have been content to stop there, to confess the ways I'd lived a false life, but if I'd learned anything about God in those times after my diagnosis, it was that he so often pushes past the easiest answers.

It's not just business, John. He was tugging at a loose thread. *What about Margaret, John? What about her opinion of you? Do you search for validation in her eyes?*

If the first question was piercing, this one was rending. Throughout our marriage, I'd worked for her approval, for her to say, "You're so good, John." I wanted her to affirm my worth, my ability. And in that need, I'd not shared my pain, the fear that I couldn't measure up. If I did, would she see me as a ten-foot-tall hero? Or, might she see me as something less, something more human? That's when it became clear—I was a slave to my own need for validation, to my need to appear strong; it was the steering force of my life. Wasn't this about my identity?

The voice came back, this time fierce with comfort.

I thought of you before I spoke the crags of West Fork into existence, or made the marmot of this valley, or speckled the river with trout. Before any of this, I thought of you. I thought of Margaret. I thought of your children, your friends, your business partners. I thought of you, created all of this for you. Your value comes from me alone.

The wind swept through the valley, sent the aspen branches waving, arms in praise.

The voice came again.

Your value is so great, I sent my Son to rescue you, to free you from your own self-sufficiency, and to teach you how to abide in my love. In him, I made you my son. Do you know how much I value my sons and daughters, John?

There it was, the family identity. I was a member of his family, a coheir with Christ in his kingdom. Why should I hide behind my masks, behind the surname of success I'd created? Could I ever create as much value as I already had in God?

And John, he said, *you have value because I say you have value. I love you without condition. You don't have to hide behind success. You don't have to try and measure up. Look to me for your value, look to me for your true identity.*

It was a moment of earnest sobriety, and everything became clearer.

I knew it was the voice of God. These things didn't sound like the ramblings of my own head. I'd never ascribed value to myself *just because.* My validation was not found in all my attempts to measure up. My validation was found only in God. I could be who I was, wholly. I could be human. I could fail, hurt, weep, laugh, whatever, and none of it would change God's love for me, the way he valued me.

A weight was being lifted, a mask, to be more precise. A freedom was coming, one I'd never known. That's the very moment I resolved to believe in this new identity of God-esteem. I'd strive no longer to receive validation by my own success and wouldn't live in false narratives of success. I wouldn't hide my weaknesses or my emotions from Margaret. I'd do only those things that allowed me to live from my true identity as a wholly imperfect, wholly known, wholly valued, and still wholly loved son of God. This would be the beginning of a new way of living; it would be the foundation for authentic living.

Didn't it change everything?

There are times when I second-guess that Cimarron experience. Had that dialogue really happened? Had I made it up? Was it some construct of my imagination? The questions come, sometimes flutter about, but I know how to shrug them off. The proof is found in the freedom.

Margaret sits beside me now, and I wonder what memories she's replaying. Maybe she's thinking about that month too. Maybe she's in other memories, replaying the thawing of our marriage from her own perspective. Perhaps she's just happy to be here, watching this movie about her husband, her family, our shared struggle. I steal a glance every now and then and know this for certain: she is beautiful.

Who knows how this would have played out if I hadn't learned to take off the masks, to live in God's validation instead of the validation of others, instead of the validation of my own making. Who knows how our relationship would have turned if I'd kept trying to live in self-sufficiency and control, if I'd kept trying to win her validation or refused to share my whole heart with her.

She is looking at the screen, eyes glassy near the corners. Are those tears? I don't know, but she's smiling. Her smile keeps me. It always has.

What a comfort Margaret became as I sank deeper into disability, as I learned to shed the false self and share my fears, pain, and emotions with her. I unhitched her from my needs for validation, authentication, and approval in those days after the Cimarron experience, and in this new way of living, I realized what Margaret always wanted most—the real, authentic, unguarded, wholehearted, disabled John Paine.

The authentic John Paine—I was moving into new territory in those days. And as it turned out, these lessons poured a sort of foundation for other lessons, lessons that might have been even harder to learn, if such a thing were possible.

CHAPTER 15

Saying Goodbye

A LS is the Delilah you never asked for. She comes to you in the night, trims your hair, leaches your strength. She exposes the little things you've always taken for granted: the coffee cup you lifted as an involuntary response to the morning, which now weighs one hundred pounds; the carpet from the bed to the bathroom, now thicker than jungle undergrowth; the thinning air; the cement-weighted diaphragm; the herculean effort of signing a document. Delilah is a devil woman.

My once-strong body was hollowing out. Four years into this disease, I shouldn't have been alive, shouldn't have been upright and able to shuffle my feet. And yet, here I was, a prisoner to my own body, which was becoming gaunter by the day. Atrophy was apparent. My shirts no longer fit at the neck. I cinched belts around my waist to keep my pants from sliding down my flattening backside. Everything was changing.

Years before, an anesthesiologist and friend, Dr. Paul Lanier, visited. He'd contracted Lou Gehrig's disease before I did, and he was well into the dance with his own Delilah. He was wheelchair bound and had employed round-the-clock caretakers. He was the living portent of my future, and he knew I was in a liminal space. I was sliding past the point of any physical competency, and Dr. Lanier was well acquainted with that slide; he understood the path that was pulling me down it. So, I sat across from him as he gave it to me straight, no chaser.

"You have to learn," he said, then paused, waiting to make sure he had my full attention, "to say goodbye."

This was a truth I did not want to hear.

"If you don't learn to say goodbye, bitterness, resentment, and depression will set in. You'll lose control of your arms, and there will be resentment. You'll lose your legs, one at a time, and the depression will come like a black cloud. Eventually all the major muscles in your body will fail. Resentment. Depression. Resentment. Depression. You can't beat this, John. You can only learn to accept it and to rise above the resentment and depression. Saying goodbye helps you move into this acceptance."

I knew it was true. I'd already lost the majority of dexterity in my hands, and walking was becoming more difficult.

"Celebrate what you still have, but begin saying goodbye before you lose it all. Hold your wife; hug your children; relish it. But prepare yourself so when that last time comes, you don't find yourself wallowing in a funk."

There we were, the two of us in the slow process of this open-air drowning, and he was teaching me how to drown with dignity and grace. This is the way of the best of friends. They share their pain so that you might learn from it. Maybe that's what it means to lay down your life for a brother.

I'd already lost the use of my left hand, but in the months that followed, the fingers of my right hand—except my thumb and forefinger—had the life sucked from them. I said goodbye to writing anything more than some preschool version of my name. More difficult, I said goodbye to holding Margaret's hand. I adapted to the changes, learned to manage more menial tasks, such as feeding myself. With great effort, I could still place my arm onto the table before sitting, and Margaret would hold the spoon between my two working right fingers. I'd pinch tight; then, arms heavy as steel beams, I'd slump over my plate and shovel food into my mouth so I didn't have to lift the spoon. It was a mess of a process, one that resulted in food dribbling down my chin. Margaret would dab my chin with a napkin, and as she did, I'd whisper, "Thank you," cheeks reddening. I wondered: Did she feel as if she were tending to a toddler again after all these years?

Ability, competency, dignity—these were the things the old John Paine fought so hard to project, the constituent parts of my identity, false though it may be from time to time. These identity puzzle pieces were disappearing, and the old John Paine was no longer recognizable. Here was God, though, making good on his promise. He was making me into something new, and this, somehow, made my slide into a second childhood more bearable, maybe even acceptable.

In the mornings, I'd say goodbye to a piece of the old John Paine; then I'd retreat into God's presence. There, I'd feel him speaking truth to my inner man, into my heart.

I said goodbye to showering myself.

You don't need to clean up to come to me, John. I love you just as you are.

I said goodbye to dressing myself.

I love you beyond your understanding, John, so much that I've clothed you in the righteousness of Christ.

I said goodbye to tending to my business in the bathroom.

Only I can validate you, John, even as you learn to accept these disabil-
ities. Now, accept yourself as I accept you—wholly.

Stripped, stripped, stripped—I was being freed of the source of any
pride. And as I was, I began to understand my true identity. I was one
with God through Christ. Because of that, I was enough. And in this
realization, what was I feeling? What was this feeling of being both
known and accepted? Could it be intimacy? Yes. That was it. Maybe this
is what Jesus meant when he spoke of the real, true, abundant, intimate
life with God.

Even as my muscles were losing their memory, my father was losing
his. He'd made his way into the latter stages of dementia, into that stage
of golden nostalgia before his mind slipped away forever. It was another
opportunity to say goodbye, but not just to the man I'd known as my
hard-nosed father. This was my chance to say goodbye to the anger,
sadness, and fear of disapproval that had driven me to perform for so
many years. This was my opportunity to forgive him just as Christ had
forgiven his accusers, just as God had forgiven me. I knew it—I could
release him, or his memory might haunt me like a ghost.

In a quiet morning of prayer, I brought my father to God. I listened
and listened until the thought came: my father had parented me from
his own wounding.

Couldn't I forgive that?

He did the best he could.

Don't we all?

He loved me, even if he didn't know how to say it.

Couldn't I see that truth?

I explored the wounds God had uncovered in the Cimarrons—the
need for validation and approval from others, the need to be seen as
competent and accomplished—and I could see it with clear eyes. Those

needs were driven by my father's unique woundings, by the way he worked those same wounds into my life. I ached for his healing and wholeness, either here or on the other side of life, and so, I asked Christ to come to the center of the pain, to heal it and fill me with love for my father.

"Fill me with forgiveness," I prayed; then I spoke the words over and over again.

"I forgive you."

"I forgive you."

"I forgive you."

As I let go of my pain and my bitterness, I understood the truth of my new identity and my father's too. I was God's child, called to forgive as he forgives; my father was God's child, worthy of God's whole, complete, unconditional love. Now, God was making a way to love my father through me as forgiveness filled my heart. God the Father was loving me so that I could love my father.

This practice of letting go, of saying goodbye—it held a secret. In it, I was coming to accept my diagnosis, my emotional pain, and even the pain my father carried. I was learning to see my life and my father's life as they were, not as I wished they were. This, I think, is what it means to be an agent of reconciliation: to see things as they are, to square up to the truth and let God bring his comfort, even in the brokenness of it all.

I'd said goodbye to so many things: climbing stairs, swimming, scratching any given itch. I'd hired a full-time driver who doubled as a part-time caretaker. The days passed into evenings, and the shape of my day-to-day life changed. I'd maintained the rhythm of my evenings, perhaps my favorite part of any day, though I knew it was only a matter of time before that changed too.

Margaret has always been an early-to-bed kind of girl, and in those days, she'd settle into bed sometime around nine o'clock each evening. She'd make her way through her typical reading charade, propping herself up on a pillow, turning on the bedside lamp, and opening a good book before dozing to sleep ten minutes later. My routine was quite different. I'd make my way to my favorite deep-cushioned chair by the bed, often reading until close to eleven. Satisfied, I'd settle into bed and fall asleep, spent. It was a good arrangement, one that worked for me. I was growing weaker, though, and with each passing night, I found myself struggling to maintain the rhythm. My arms now dead, Margaret would open my book, set it in my lap, and place my hands on either side. With my right thumb and forefinger, I'd turn the pages with great care, sliding the edge under the fingers of my resting left hand. It was a tedious process and grew more tedious by the day. When I was finished, I'd stand, shuffle to the bed where Margaret had pulled the covers back, and with a series of arm slings and knee raises, I'd pull the covers over my chest before falling to sleep. It was unconventional, but isn't so much about adapting to death?

It was a night like any other, though I should have seen it coming. The routine had been the same—the chair, the book, the pulled-back covers. Having had my fill of reading, I stood, allowed the book to fall from my lap to the floor. I dragged to the bed, then stretched myself under the covers. I tried to sling my arms up using my knees, tried to throw the covers over my chest; I couldn't. It was no use; I couldn't cover myself.

I turned to look at Margaret, already asleep, and there was no way I would wake that kind of resting peace. Pity set in—self-pity is a difficult battle for the ALS patient—as I realized there was no feasible way to solve this problem. In that pity, I was overcome by emotion. Tomorrow night, would I have to turn in with Margaret? Would I have to let her tuck me in and turn off the lights? Would I stare up at the dark ceiling, unable to move until I was able to fall asleep hours later? Did I have to say goodbye to my favorite part of the day?

I rolled to my side and climbed out of bed, arms dangling. I shuffled back to the chair I'd just left and sat in fresh awareness of my newest loss. Why tonight? Why ever, really?

I felt the sadness and resentment and depression creeping in, knew that this kind of self-pity made life so much darker, so I turned to prayer. I waited for an answer, a sense, anything. I heard nothing. I waited, started praying again, and that's when a movie started playing in my mind's eye. It was the video of my life. I was a young boy in Tyler, running from home, pushing past the boundaries my parents had set. I was a college student in love, but I was spending more time away from Margaret, more time pursuing academic achievement. I was married, working for Mr. Hill, and asserting my independence more and more. I was a successful builder, an entrepreneur, a self-made man. I was sitting in the doctor's office, the recipient of a terminal diagnosis, and even in my success, I felt so alone. Where were my parents? Where was Mr. Hill? Where was Margaret, really? They were a part of my life, sure, but were they *in* it? Were we connected in intimacy, connected in such a way that would help me carry the load? Hadn't all my assertions of independence been nothing more than acts of isolation?

That's when I felt the words, flooding.

I created you for dependence on me and others. Your pursuit of independence pushed all of us to arm's length. Say goodbye to independence. Really.

Conviction is a difficult thing. First, he'd convicted me of my understanding of his love, then of ways I sought validation. Now he was showing me that dependence was not weakness, so long as I was dependent on the right things. And just as it had in those other moments, this new moment of conviction brought a sorrow with it. This false independence, all this striving to prove my self-sufficiency—what was it worth? How had I missed this truth, that God created us for proper dependence? I knew it at once—the false John Paine had made this kind of dependence impossible. How could I confess my failures, my weaknesses, my inadequacies, if I needed others to believe that I had the answer to every problem? To admit I needed others would require an act of transparency, of confession. Wouldn't it?

It was a moment triggered by the silliest thing—my inability to cover up—but it exposed a deeper, longer trend. Now I felt myself invited into something new: the admission of my need for others was necessary if I was to kill the false man. Only through this death of the false man could I plumb the depths of intimacy.

I will care for you as you learn to give in, I heard in that moment. *I have you covered.*

I'd learned to trust these inklings, these deeper leadings of God, and so, I stood from my chair and made my way back to my bed. I scooted my feet under the covers again and waited for something to happen. Margaret stirred, raised up on her elbow, and pulled the covers up over me. She lay back down, still sound asleep.

"Margaret?" I whispered.

No answer.

"Margaret?"

Still no answer.

"Thank you, Lord," I prayed into the dark.

The next morning, I thanked Margaret for covering me, but she didn't remember any of it. She'd slept straight through the night, she said, shrugging. It was a little thing, maybe, but it was the thing I needed. I needed to learn how resting in proper dependence makes a way for the work of God.

I consider the lesson of that night—intimacy and dependence go hand in hand. And what is dependence but the offspring of courage and trust? As the nights wore on, I learned to exercise that courage and trust, and without fail, Margaret covered me, even as she slept. It was a sign meant for me, the way God and Margaret operated in tandem to provide the simplest act of care.

It was God.

It was also Margaret.

Wasn't it always Margaret and God?

Together, they were teaching me the truth of Scripture: the power of God—his intimate interaction with us—is made perfect in our weakness.

———✕———

Sometimes I wonder if all those years of living into a false narrative and wearing masks broke something in me. This art of learning to say good-bye, of learning to lean into dependence upon God and others, becomes more natural, but it's still so difficult. Even now, in the spiritual high of this theater, it's difficult. Will I ever learn it?

The spot that was hurting me yesterday is kicking my butt tonight. In fact, the spot is on my butt, the left cheek, to be exact, and it feels as if an ice pick is poking straight through it, up into the bone. I ask Leo to lean me back a bit more, and he does. The pain doesn't go away, but it shifts up and into a different part of my left cheek. Somehow, this helps.

"Thanks, Leo," I whisper into the dark, but he cannot hear me.

The movie plays and for the first time, I notice how loud it seems. I can feel my nerves fraying and becoming hyperaware. Oversensitivity works into all my senses, an aggravating byproduct of ALS.

I focus elsewhere, concentrate on my breathing. The ventilator pushes air into my lungs. I give in to the rhythm, purse my lips when the ventilator pushes air through my nose. If I do not close my mouth, all that air pushed through my nostrils comes wheezing out of my mouth. Dependence upon this machine requires that I give in to the rhythm, that I do my part. I suppose a day will come when the muscles around my lips will quiver, and those fasciculations will be an omen, a portent. If I can't purse my lips, I'll have nothing to offer and the ventilator will be useless. On that day, death waits for me. Heaven too. I suppose one act of dependency gives way to another, and another, and another, until we leak out of this life and into an eternity of proper, dependent connection with God. All of this—I guess it's training for the life to come. It's dying to live.

I smile considering this. Every goodbye is just a transition, just an opportunity for some new hello.

I look at the screen as the faces of my family flash, and flash, and flash. My lips quiver, but this isn't the death omen. This is something different. Life—it is so beautiful, even in the dying. I whisper a gentle farewell. It's the same farewell I whisper almost every night.

CHAPTER 16

Freedom Through Emotions

I t'd been years since my deathnosis, and that's when it struck me—
I'd come into the beauty of the relationship I'd imagined when I
said, "I do." I was coming into an intimacy with God that I didn't know
was possible too. The days were a physical grind, each a little more difficult than the last. My deepening connectedness to God and Margaret
made my life fuller than it'd ever been, though. This was the kind of
fullness I'd always hoped for. Why had it taken so much pain to find it?

Pain is never pleasant, but I suppose this much can be said about
it: it can be made into something useful if it brings you to the end of
yourself.

I was losing my ability to walk or even stand for any period of time.
I'd found Leo, my office assistant and caretaker. I was sitting more and
more, and I'd made peace with my waning mobility. When my legs
tired out, I resorted to a push wheelchair, though I'd already purchased
an electric wheelchair, which I kept in storage for the coming inevitability. These were the twilight days. Would I be wheelchair-bound in two

weeks, two months, ten months? I didn't know, but at the present clip, I knew it'd be sooner rather than later. Before that day came, I wanted one last beach vacation, one last group of evenings watching the sunset over the ocean with Margaret. We'd stand there, her holding me as I willed myself upright. We'd set a memory in concrete. I needed this. She needed it too.

It was Father's Day when we arrived at our beachfront condo in Florida, and after unpacking for the week, Margaret busied herself with dinner in the kitchen. I'd tried to call my father earlier in the day, but he hadn't answered. My health was failing. His was too. I didn't want to let this Father's Day slip by without speaking with him, times being what they were, and just as Margaret was pulling lasagna from the oven, my phone rang. Earpiece in, I asked Margaret to answer, and she did, though with a sideways glance of hesitation. As I spoke to my father on the balcony overlooking the ocean, as I tried my best to cut through his dementia and show him the love I'd been learning, Margaret simmered. She stormed in and out of the sliding storm door, setting the balcony table with no small amount of force. She all but threw the silverware down and dropped the casserole dish in the center. She sat in a huff, tapping her fingers on the glass top of the table.

I turned to her, mouthed, "Is there a problem?"

"It's just time for dinner," she said, perhaps louder than she needed to.

With that, my blood boiled, and I imagined throwing the dishes from the balcony (if only I could). I could see them floating, as if in slow motion, seagulls trying to catch bits of noodles in midair. I envisioned the plates crashing on the picnic tables fifteen stories below, saw them shatter, and in that moment, I knew the conversation with my father was over. I took a deep breath, said my goodbye, and turned to Margaret.

"Honey, excuse me, but I need to take a walk."

She protested, tried to apologize, and though I accepted her apology, I said I still needed some time to cool down.

"This is not about you, Margaret. It's about me. I need to sort out my emotions."

I couldn't make it far in those days, but I could still swing my arm up and allow my hand to crash down on a lever-style door handle. I could still hook my hand through the lever, could still force it open. I could still walk as far as the elevator, could still manage to swing my arm high enough to punch the ground-floor button with a nubby knuckle until it lit up. I could shuffle the short distance to the picnic tables just past the parking lot, the tables where I'd imagined the dishes smashing. I could make it no farther. I sat there, watching the shadows lengthen across the beach and wondered how this, the first of our last beach evenings, had spun so out of control. I considered the heat in my cheeks, the burning in my stomach. This was pure anger.

Margaret—hadn't she been unfair to set limits on my time with my father, especially in these waning years of his lucidity? We didn't talk often, and I needed just a little time with him. It was Father's Day, after all. Shouldn't she be willing to sacrifice a little time on the only day set aside for my dad?

The fire set in, the wave of raw emotion. I wondered—why had this little thing sent me reeling in so much anger? Anger, anger, anger. I wasn't well practiced expressing anger in those days. It was a negative emotion, one of those I'd taught myself to control, to push down. But now, as I was learning to kill the false man, as I was becoming more practiced with the awakening that was happening in my heart, all my emotions felt more powerful, perhaps important. This anger was no exception. Why had it taken such hold? There, I felt the familiar tug, then the voice.

Your anger—it's about fairness, he said.

I sat at that table, listened to the waves pounding the sand. My anger pounded too, and I considered this word—*fairness*. Didn't I believe myself to be a pretty good fella, a fair fella, a person worthy of receiving a fair shake? And yet, Margaret, God, the world, no one seemed to be capitulating. How long had I felt this way? I asked God to guide me, asked him to help me trace a line back, and back, and back until it was clear: I'd always believed that life should be fair, that it should compensate me for my hard work, my fair shake. But the world proved to be pretty unfair. As a boy, my father stomped through the house on many occasions, demanding that the world adjust to his schedule. Wasn't he always unfair in his treatment of me, the way he criticized me, the demands he made of me? And what about Margaret? Had she ever been fair in her criticism of me, how much time I spent working, or ministering, or whatever? I was only trying to provide for her, for the children—at least, that's what I'd told myself. Was it fair that I'd lost my construction business and then my consumer products business? Was it fair that I'd almost lost a daughter to a disease, that there were so many years of struggle against that disease? And then there was this diagnosis.

The diagnosis. Margaret.

Margaret. The diagnosis.

It was a slow epiphany.

Was my diagnosis fair to Margaret? It was a sobering thought. Maybe she'd not been given a fair shake, either. And beyond the diagnosis, had I always been fair to her? For years, I'd taken calls at dinner, always squeezed business in at the margins. To Margaret, this must have felt like just one more slight, one more indication that everyone else, every other deal, was more important than she was. Was that fair? Maybe the steam had been building in her. Maybe she felt as though I'd always robbed her of time, as though I was robbing her of what little time we had left by prioritizing my father over her. I considered the thought, and it stung.

"God, I don't want to live this way," I prayed, and that's when I remembered Jesus. He knew a thing or two about being treated unfairly, I supposed, yet he didn't resort to anger and self-pity. He could have imposed his notions of fairness on others, could have smitten the men who murdered him. Instead, he lived from his core identity as the most loved Son of God, the Chief Reconciler of the world. In that identity, he traded his life for the life of the world—an unfair bargain if ever there was one.

It was a moment of great clarity. God was using my anger—this negative emotion—to expose a secret belief and to show how it was so at odds with the life Christ lived. There was nothing left but to repent.

"I'm sorry, God. Come into this anger and heal it."

That's all it took. The anger melted, and though my legs were full of lead, I felt light as air. I made my way back to the fifteenth floor and walked into the condominium. There was Margaret, sitting at the table with an empty plate in front of her, the corners of her lips turned down. I explained the root of my anger, told her I felt as if everything was so unfair. But then I apologized and told her I realized how unfair I'd been for so long.

"You're the most important person in the world to me," I said, "and I love you. I don't want to fight this week. You are my priority."

She reached across the table and took my hand. She forgave me. I forgave her. The air cleared.

Intimacy: Is it possible without sitting in our emotions, without allowing them to lead us to our secrets? Is it possible without wrestling down those secrets, without seeing the truth behind them? Is it possible without owning our part in the messes of our world, the messes of our relationships, all the messes of our own making?

I was learning to walk in the fullness of my emotions, which was no small task. After years of ignoring them, of pushing them down, any feeling was almost too much. But as I learned to root into the experience of my emotions, as I learned to examine what was beneath those emotions, I found God was unwinding false beliefs. He was making me into something new, something more tender, more authentic.

We left Florida and made our way back to Texas for a few weeks before heading to the Cimarron Mountains. Colorado had become our summer nest after that first monthlong retreat. The air was cooler, more arid, and somehow seemed easier to breathe. Life was slower there, too, and it gave me space to reflect, to explore the progression of my disease, and to connect with God in that exploration.

My diaphragm was losing strength, my neck growing weaker.

God, be my strength.

I still had the use of one index finger, and if Margaret wrapped my arms around her, I could still manage something resembling a hug.

Lord, hug her when I can't.

I was finding my way into the wheelchair more and more, though I'd walk as often as I could, some days farther than others.

God, teach me to walk in your ways, even as I'm confined to this chair.

Early autumn set in, and we were just a week from our return to Dallas. I was scheduled to be the keynote speaker at a men's retreat a few weeks after my return, and I'd not spent time preparing the way I should have. The aspen leaves began their turning, their yellowing, and I followed suit. Those old voices came creeping back.

What if I wasn't prepared enough, the way I always was?

What if I couldn't deliver something poignant?

What if they didn't respond to my message?

What if it wasn't as polished as it needed to be?

The days were slipping by, and what was this emotion that was creeping in? Was it fear? Was it anxiety?

I told Margaret I needed to gather my thoughts and get some notes prepared for the retreat. We decided that the pass at West Fork would be the perfect place for me to work, and Margaret could spend her own time in the beauty of nature. She could read, pray, perhaps walk a trail or two. Again, we loaded onto the four-wheeler, Margaret taking the driver's seat. Again, we made the one-hour jaunt. Again, Margaret set up my chair. Again, I sat there holding my ulterior motives as best as I could in failing hands. But as I sat in that chair, here came the fear and anxiety again. Why?

I closed my eyes and asked God for help to see. I tried to reach past my feelings, hoped to stretch into some inspirational epiphany to share with the men at the upcoming retreat. Before I found a handhold in those mountains, though, the voice of God changed the conversation, as the voice of God is wont to do.

Are you enjoying my creation?

What kind of question was that? Wasn't I here, looking for inspiration in the crevices of these mountains, in the sunbeams splitting the clouds? All I wanted was to get a few things organized, to finish a little work for God before giving in to full enjoyment. All I wanted was to prepare past the anxiety, prepare to the point where I knew I could deliver.

"Let me get these few things done; let me get the work finished, then I'll turn to enjoyment in full," I said. I closed my eyes, waiting for some retreat-worthy epiphany.

John, are you enjoying the wife I've given you?

I imagined Margaret sitting by her favorite stream. She was fine. Wasn't she? And yes, I'd enjoy her just as soon as I got a little more work finished. I reminded God of the importance of this retreat, these men. This was his work, after all, wasn't it?

John, are you enjoying me?

I'd tried my best to shake these voices, to ignore a God who wanted nothing more than to release me from my own fear trap of performance, but he would not be ignored. Was I enjoying him? The truth is, I wasn't, really. And why? It was the anxiety. I turned to my emotions, examined them. What was behind it? Duty? Not quite. Perfection? Yes, that's the stuff. And what drove that need for perfection?

The sun lit up the valley, and I was sitting in the glory of these mountains, the glory of my own epiphany too. I'd gotten lost in hero complexes again, in my own ego. And though there's nothing wrong with wanting to do a good job, this was something more taxing. I was trying to craft the message that might prove me to be some sort of spiritual giant. I was playing in validation motifs again. The need for validation from others is a hard habit to kick, I suppose, and my kicking muscles were proving quite weak.

I considered my history, this time turning to the root of my fear of failure and imperfection. Where was it?

Over the years, I'd found that perfect performances garnered the praises of men, and it was the perfection that made me feel so worthy, so validated, so loved. But it was this same self-sufficient perfection that disrupted my intimate dependence upon God and my understanding of his love. There, in that emotional torrent, I began to put the pieces together, maybe for the first time.

Understand God's wild, unwieldy, unmerited, unconditional love.

Yes.

Understand how his love alone validates me, how being grafted into this love is the only thing that establishes my worth and identity.

Yes.

Understand my inability to graft myself into that love; understand how only he can graft me into it.

Yes.

Understand how to rest in dependency upon this love he imparts, this validation.

Yes.

Be honest with my emotions; allow those emotions to teach me the ways I lose sight of his love and validation when things don't seem fair to me.

Yes.

The wind blew against my cheeks, and I felt it waking me. If I could live from these truths, I could stay connected to God's presence, to his love. I could see him in the world around me, could be ever awake to his gifts, to his perspectives. Gifts like these mountains. Gifts like Margaret. Even when there were things to do, God didn't need me striving after perfection in the performance of those things. He was more concerned that I learn to be with him, to enjoy him. What is intimacy without enjoyment, after all?

I stood, as carefully as I could. It was a slow slog down to the place where Margaret was sitting, the path uneven and rocky and my footing being so uncertain. It was a trek that should have taken a few minutes, but now, the path seemed infinite. I saw Margaret from the back, and as I approached her, quieter than a field mouse, I offered a prayer of contrition. We were all here, together—God, Margaret, and me—and I wouldn't lose this rare moment to work. I whispered my amen, now just feet away from Margaret, and she looked up, surprised to see me.

"What are you doing here?" she asked, knowing I couldn't be finished preparing.

I smiled, told her I decided to come and be with her.

"Instead of working, let's just have some fun," I told her. She looked at me, gape-mouthed at first, then smiling.

We sat beside the stream—her favorite sitting spot—and we talked. I shared about my encounter with God, how he'd told me to quit working, to enjoy him, his creation, and her. She laughed and handed me the spiral-bound notebook in her lap. She had written a near-verbatim recitation of those same words—words God had spoken to her as he was speaking them to me.

She leaned against my shoulder and stretched her arm around my back, both pressing into me and holding me up. I sat, arms dangling at my side. We sat just like that, in silence, reveling in the incredible gift of a synchronized grace. Minutes passed, maybe an hour. Margaret stood, helped me up, and we climbed back onto the four-wheeler. She wrapped my arms around her waist, and I squeezed as best I could. We drove up to the trailhead, taking in the fullness of God's beauty. We watched as the low sun seemed to bleach the evergreen trunks, as the wind roused the aspen leaves from rest. We stopped at every overlook, and Margaret cut the engine so we could hear the birds sing their autumn songs. Had we almost lost this moment to my stubborn penchant for perfectionism?

A few weeks later, I met with those men, and I was unprepared—at least, according to the standards of the old John Paine. I wasn't accustomed to winging it, but what else was there to do? Somehow, even in that winging, even in all the glory of its imperfection, I felt at ease. Inspiration had come. In fact, I felt at one with God, sustained by him, enjoying him, even in the spontaneity of it all. I suppose this is the kind of oneness that comes with intimacy.

The emotions—fear, anger, anxiety, even sorrow—aren't they an essential part of being? Aren't they gateways to our deeper beliefs, gateways into the heart? I know, now, how my anger flares when I think things aren't fair, how the anxiety rises when I turn back toward self-sufficiency, independence, and seeking validation from others. But if I sit with these emotions, if I bring them to God, he'll come with his counsel, healing, and comfort. He'll draw me into his presence. He uses our emotions to draw us into intimacy, if only we'll let him.

It's become clearer in these last days. I so often distanced myself from emotional honesty and vulnerability, and by that, I pushed God to arm's length too. I created a span that made true intimacy impossible. How I wish I would have known this all those years ago. Perhaps I'd have lived a different path. But all the maybes and perhaps in the world cannot release me from the history I've lived. All I know now is this present experience of God and his gifts.

Gifts like the joy of this moment.

Gifts like the peace of his presence, even in this theater.

Gifts like contentment in the nightmare of this paralysis.

Gifts like the faith, hope, love, and joy that brighten the darkest hours.

Gifts like the people in this theater.

It is all a grace, and all that grace makes me smile.

CHAPTER 17

The Standing Invitation

Twelve years into the violence of my disease, everything felt unnatural.

The disease had consumed my arms, both hands, my legs, and my feet. The atrophy had spread to my core muscles, and sitting up was becoming more difficult. I spent the majority of my days in the motorized wheelchair, but when the fire set into my hindquarters, when it became unbearable, my full-time caretakers—Leo during the day, others overnight and during the morning hours—helped me stand, relieving some of the pressure. Legs straightened, leaning against a counter, I still had enough core strength to balance the weight over my hip joints. It was a tiny freedom, but in this stage of my disease, even the tiniest freedom is sweet.

As I lost much of my mobility, my circulation slowed. By the end of any given day, blood pooled in my hands and feet. This swelling—edema, my doctors called it—brought with it an enduring chill, a sort of endless winter. Those were the days when I began wearing long sleeves, jackets, and sometimes light gloves, even in the summer months.

Years of experimental intravenous immunoglobulin treatments had left my veins fried and brittle. Even the most skilled nurses found it difficult to run IVs or take blood as my spent veins rolled away from any given needle. So, the doctors installed a subclavian port, a sort of access point mounted just below the chest with a tube attached that ran through my chest. The port provided my medical team with direct access to the largest vein in my chest so they could draw blood and administer antibiotics. What was convenient for them was hell for me. The hardened neoprene port head rubbed against the sensitive skin on my chest, and when I was wearing a shirt, it sometimes pressed against my ribs with a sort of piercing discomfort.

I'd lost so much of my diaphragmatic capacity that I'd begun intermittent use of the ventilator. The doctors taught me to sync my breathing with it, to purse my lips as it pressed air into my lungs. It was difficult to cede control of breathing in those early days, especially when I had something to say. I'd fall out of rhythm with the machine, and as I tried to speak during the mechanical inhalation, I felt as if I were drowning on air. In time, though, I learned to relax when it inhaled for me and to speak when it allowed me to exhale. In the mornings, when I felt strong and capable, I'd do my best to breathe *au naturel*. By the afternoons, though, breathing was a chore, and on most days, I'd resort to the use of the ventilator. At night, it was a foregone conclusion. I could use the BiPAP or risk falling asleep and waking into eternity. Nocturnal suffocation—this is one of the ever-present risks of ALS.

Twelve years in. How had I made it so long?

In my last days of mobility, I was recovering from a surgery to replace the port in my chest. The skin around my previous port had adhered to the neoprene surface just below the skin. The port was accessed with a twenty-two-gauge L-shaped needle that penetrated the skin all day, every day. As that skin lost blood flow due to the constant needle penetration, it became necrotic; it blackened, died, and pulled away from the round port head, leaving a half-inch-diameter hole in my chest. These sorts of holes can lead to infection—a life-threatening prospect to an ALS patient—and so, a new port had been placed just above the first rib on my right side.

It was the morning after the surgery to install the new port, and I lay in bed, nauseated and groggy. I called to my overnight caretaker and asked him to help me transfer to my wheelchair. Perhaps some time at the office would help clear the cobwebs. Maybe a bit of movement would pump some life back into me. It might be a good idea to rest, Margaret had suggested, but I knew better. There were things to do, decisions to make, and I loved my ministry work.

The work of a dying man—when does it end?

Transfer made, I wheeled into the bathroom, where my caretaker helped me stand. I turned backward, rested my butt on the top of the bathroom vanity, and sat upright as he straightened my legs and positioned them on the floor. I settled as much weight as I could over my hips and strained to keep my torso upright. Still wearing the hospital socks from the day before, I noticed the tacky dots on the bottom were dust covered and no longer quite so tacky. It was a passing thought, an unimportant detail. It was the sort of detail, though, you wished you had paid attention to after the accident. But hadn't I stood just like this a hundred times before?

My caretaker turned to my closet, considering what clothes I might wear for the day. No sooner had he taken his eyes off me than I felt my feet sliding on the travertine floor. First my left. Then my right. As they began to spread the wrong way, my butt slipped off the granite top. Weight was being transferred to my legs, and those dead legs were no longer fit for load bearing.

I'd suffered through more than one spill as my legs were giving out on me, and if there's one thing I knew, it was this: there is a moment of epiphany that precedes every fall, and in that moment, the questions flood. These were the questions before this one, the fall of falls:

What if I'd listened to Margaret?

Wouldn't I still be in bed?

Why didn't I pay closer attention to the details, the slippery socks?

Is there a way to land without breaking?

Can I go back and start this day over?

This was it—the big one. I knew it even before I could call out to my caretaker. On my way down, I felt my knee buckle then snap backward, a rubber band breaking. My weight now unsupported, I fell straight down, and my left leg folded underneath me. As the full weight of my body landed on top of my leg, there was an audible pop as my leg contorted ninety degrees and splayed out underneath and then past my right hip. A shot of pain blazed a trail from my hip to my brain, and my head smashed against the travertine, splitting the crown. That's when the chemical rush came, and the brief euphoria of shock set in just before the nausea. Blood pooled under my cheek, warming the cold travertine. I noticed it, then didn't. I noticed it again, fading in from black as my caretaker tried to straighten the leg that was folded in an anatomical impossibility.

This was a pain I'd never experienced. It was fire, and needles, and electricity, and the full-body shiver of too much blood draining. It was a swelling pain and a hollow pain too. It was hunger, maybe even starvation. It was too deep an itch and too deep a scratch. It was cat claws and snakebite. It was a drill bit biting my hip, boring through my pelvic bone. It was every pain under the sun, even the pain of the sun.

The paramedics carried me to the ambulance, screaming.

I asked the first responders for morphine, for any narcotic to kill this heat burning just behind my eyes. There was a frantic attempt to hit a vein. No dice.

"The port!" I screamed, and they tore open my shirt, as if they intended to do something.

"I'm sorry, Mr. Paine. We're not allowed to access it."

Strapped to a gurney, which was bolted to the ambulance, there was a gentle sway that rocked pain into the bones I knew were broken. Where was the presence of God in this pain? What about his comforting presence? And if he wouldn't come with his presence, couldn't he at least have provided me with some morphine? Why had I been left to these incompetent first responders?

A group of doctors met us at the doors to the emergency room, and one attached my port to a bag of morphine. A slow warmth set in, as if I were being covered in heavy fleece. I was falling into a warm hole, into darkness, into something approximating a waking dream.

I went in and out of consciousness, aware that Margaret was there. There was some discussion of surgery, and did one of the doctors say something about risk, something about ALS patients going under and never waking up? I remember one surgeon discussing my depressed respiration rate, telling Margaret that anesthesia would depress it even further. I recall the surgeon speaking to me, his voice coming as if down a long tunnel. The head of my femur had snapped and was free-floating in my hip socket, he said. The ligaments around my knee were ripped through too. The bones of my knee were broken. Surgical intervention was necessary. There was no other option.

In the hours before surgery, I drifted in and out of a morphine-induced euphoria. In a lucid moment, I remember the surgeons talking with the pulmonologist from the ALS clinic on the speakerphone. Anesthesia posed too high a risk, he said, and so, it was decided that I'd receive an epidural to block the nerves below my waist, and I'd stay awake through the surgery.

In another lucid moment, I called Margaret and my children to my bed. "Please remember this," I said. "The greatest treasure in life is intimacy with God. It's possible. Don't ever quit pursuing it."

The nurses came to prep me for surgery. I felt a pinprick in my spine, then every sensation below my waist melted, or floated away, or evaporated. I'd lost my legs, and what if the feeling spread upward? Was this what dying felt like? Would I ever speak lucid words to my Margaret, to my children, again?

I wondered whether I'd made the most of this life. I wondered whether I'd sorted out the experience of God. I wondered, and wondered, and wondered until a peace settled in, and as it did, I knew it: even in this, all would be well.

What is pain if not an invitation to know your frailty? What is pain if not an invitation to die to your own comfort? What is pain if not an invitation to die altogether?

In the months after my surgery, the pain was excruciating. The doctors limited my access to painkillers because chronic use of narcotics depresses respiration. The pain was buried beneath my skin; it was marrow deep. I wondered how much longer this sort of living was possible. Even in prayer, even knowing the love of God, there was no relief. These were the first days of the maddening pain. These were the days I began to pray in earnest, "Lord, take me home."

In the clinic, I met with a specialist who was familiar with my case. There were ways to deal with this pain, he said. I was on mechanized life support, and since I had already signed a "do not resuscitate" order, I could check into the clinic and be hooked up to a morphine drip. I could take one last kiss from my Margaret and pray a final blessing over my children. As the chemical warmth set in, I could give a simple nod to the medical team and they could remove the ventilator. I could fall into a peaceful, eternal sleep. It was my ticket home, but there was no reason to make any sudden decisions. This was a standing invitation, he said.

A standing invitation to die. Why did this thought spark joy in my heart?

I weighed the options. I spoke with Margaret and a few trusted friends. It was an enticing offer, one that promised release. But as I brought this to God at the start of every day, as I let him know that this could be my ticket out, the voice came, booming like thunder.

Control again? He asked, reminding me that this was ground we'd already covered. It was true, I confessed. I wanted to be in control of my own pain. I wanted to make the ultimate call that would end this burning. I didn't want to trust; I didn't want to fight this anymore. I only wanted release.

Trust me, I heard. *Be with me.*

With.

This was the word, and when I heard it, I remembered a conversation with a close friend. He'd been explaining his prayer practices to me just months before, and he'd asked a poignant question.

"Did you know that God created us to be visual creatures? Did you know you can use visualization as a way to experience the presence of God, even in the pain?"

"How does it work?" I asked.

"When the pain comes, find a quiet place. Close your eyes. Imagine Christ with you, beside you in the pain. See him in your mind's eye. Feel his touch. Hear his words. See what happens."

It was a new practice, one outside the box of my conservative theology. But what did I have to lose? If anything could help, couldn't it be Jesus?

Yes. Let it be Jesus.

I practiced every time the pain set in, and as the weeks passed, it became easier to visualize God with me, my *Immanuel*. Many days I imagined myself in the woods beside Lake Palestine. There, I'd sit on a stump, and I'd see my Jesus sitting on another stump across from me. I'd open up to him, bare my pain to him. It was a vulnerable practice, a practice of desperation. But as I confessed my pain, my want of death, I could almost feel his hands on the places of my pain. I could sense the warmth of his presence. As I stretched further into visualization, I could hear his words like Scripture.

I am your refuge and strength, your very present help in time of need. My compassions never fail. They are new every morning. My faithfulness endures forever.

Sitting in the pain and being honest with it, vulnerable with it—as I'd learned to be with my emotions—I began trusting my healer even more. With each passing day of practice, I began to sense that this deteriorating body—this pain-filled, paralyzed body—was not the real me. The real me, the spiritual me, was somewhere behind the eyes, somewhere more interior. The real me could meet with God in the paradise he'd planted in my deepest parts. And all I had to do to meet him there was release myself to his rhythm. As he visited, he poured his love into me, his validation, and with it came his joy and peace too. With it came contentment. My job in those moments was simple: I was to receive, receive, receive. In my pain, my weakness, my powerlessness, he gave me the grace to receive.

I met with God day after day, and as I did, the appeal of my standing invitation to die lost its luster. I no longer went to God to escape my pain, but instead, I went to him because of my great affection for him. Every day was a new day with my Father, a new day to hear his voice and to trust it. Every day was a new day to learn his love and to love him back.

Do you have any idea the depths of my love for you today?

"I think I'm starting to understand," I'd say.

Good. Trust it to be true. Share it with Margaret. Share it with your children. Share it with Leo, with your business partners. Share it with the world.

The days turned to months, and the months stacked up, turned into a year, then a second year. I found myself asking a simple question: Why was I still here? Was it because I didn't feel release? Was it because of some moral obligation to fight to the end? Was it because of some inherent objection to intentional death? I don't suppose it was any of those things. Instead, over time, I've learned to put it this way: I serve at the pleasure of my Master. My Master still has more to teach me about his love, and he wants me to spread more of his love to Margaret, to my children, grandchildren, and friends. How do I know? Because he's told me.

I'm a dead man, a man whose soul is tethered to his body by way of artificial means. Where would I be without this ventilator? My diaphragm would collapse; my lungs would deflate.

Where would I be without this port through which so many of my medications are delivered? The motor neurons would become inflamed and my muscular function would disappear. Infection would eat me from the inside out.

How would I function without this chair, without the apparatus to pump blood from my feet to my legs at night, without all this medication? I'd be long gone, shining into the golden gleam of forever.

The movie is coming to a close, and even now, I consider how the credits of my life are coming too. Within the last year, I've entered a new season of transition. It's becoming more difficult to swallow, and getting any bite of food down takes three, four, maybe five attempts. There are times the food sticks to the ribs, hanging up midway down the esophagus. If swallowing becomes an impossibility, the doctors will recommend the insertion of a feeding tube. But is life worth living without the sense of taste? Without coffee, wine, or chocolate cake?

I serve at the pleasure of my Master.

My diaphragm grows weaker by the day; my lips too. A day is coming, perhaps soon, when breathing will take too much labor. When that happens, I'll know the end is near. I've spoken with God about this, about the prospect of suffocating to death. There is fear, I've told him, but not in the death. The fear is in the physicality of the process. I've shared this fear with God, and in it, I've felt a great peace.

I serve at the pleasure of my Master.

I've opened up to Margaret about all of this too. I've told her a day may come when I can no longer speak, when a stroke may rob me of any ability to communicate. A day may come when machines are the only thing keeping me alive. I may ask her to call the caretaker, to load me up in the van, to take me to the clinic and instigate the pain-management protocol that would surely end my life. I've laid myself bare in this conversation, have asked her to trust me on that day. She's been vulnerable with me too. She's told me how hard it will be when that time comes, but even still, she'll trust. She's made peace with that.

We've learned the art of vulnerability and trust with our God and with each other. Here, with the movie credits rolling, I consider that vulnerability and trust.

Aren't these the ultimate proofs of intimacy?

Yes, I think that's true.

In this intimacy, I'll continue until I can continue no more. When the day of release comes, I'll be transported into forever. There, I'll see my heavenly Father face-to-face, not through the lens of inner imagination, not through a mirror dimly. Beaming, excited, I'll tell him I did my best to serve at his pleasure. Perhaps I'll add this too: "Sorry it took me so long."

CHAPTER 18

Between Waking and Dreaming

Fifty-three minutes have passed since the first light flickered on the screen, and interview outtakes play to the right of the rolling credits. I'm squinting, though I hadn't realized it before now. My eyes are burning from the salt in the corners, and my nose is running. My upper lip is slick—there is no delicate way to put this—and the trickle from my nose has disrupted the seal on my nasal pillow. I can feel the air pushing from the nozzle, spraying just outside my nose, just outside the reach of my lungs. I'm grasping, gasping, but not for long. I feel the hurried but deliberate hand of Leo, pressing a handkerchief to my nose. He wipes the corners of my eyes first, then my nose. He pushes the nozzle of my ventilator back into place, and I feel the seal.

Breathing again, I come into the present and I can hear the crowd. There is sniffling and nose blowing. They have come to the end of this evening, the evening celebrating my journey. I hope, though, that they are coming into a journey of their own. I hope they are coming into the presence of the God who wants nothing more than intimacy with them.

The truth, as painful as it is to swallow, is that so many of them will go back to the distractions of the day-to-day grind, back to the schedules, tasks, and to-dos. They'll go back to their search for wealth, or striving for the approval of others, or maybe even legacy. So many will return to their self-sufficiency complexes and mechanisms of validation. They'll go back thinking, what? Success and significance will give them something they didn't give me? Something they've never given anyone else? They'll believe they're somehow different from all of us who've come to the end of our lives knowing the truth?

And this is the truth: real living is found in intimate connection to God, to ourselves, to others, and to the world around us.

I wonder about the story of my study on that first night of my diagnosis. Will this crowd carry it with them? Will they internalize it? Will they come to know the God who wants nothing more than to visit them in their darkest day? Will they search for the God who wants nothing more than to love them without condition, just as they are, even in their brokenness, failure, or inability? This is the God I know. It's the One I want them to know too.

Maybe you'd draw just a few, Lord? I pray, and that's exactly what I mean. This disease has made me realistic if anything. There are some, I know, who aren't ready for this message. Maybe they haven't been wrecked enough yet. Maybe they've not learned to be still enough. Maybe it's just not God's timing. Who knows, but I believe this much: God wants everyone to know his love, his intimacy, the Jesus who made it possible for us to experience these things.

All in good time, I pray.

The tears are welling up again, and even here, I sit with these emotions. I am grateful for the few who might listen; I am sorrowful for those who will not, but hopeful that they will come around. More than any of this, I am grateful that God chose my weakness to invite others into this journey of intimacy.

I close my eyes and sense the still, small voice. I can almost hear it—*Well done*. I know this waxing of the Spirit; it is the waxing of love. *Thank you, Lord*.

Leo works my face over again with the rag. Then I hear him stuff it back into the plastic sandwich bag, push it into the backpack attached to my chair, and zip it closed. We're a good team, Leo and me. One day, I hope the world will know how much he's done for me, how well he's cared for me. He'll be such an asset to someone else when I'm gone.

Leo looks at me, asks me if I'm all right. I tell him that we need to move. It has been a long day, much longer than I'm accustomed to, and lava is running through the veins on my lower thighs. The devil's pitchfork has been lodged in my back for this last hour, and one of the tines now runs through my shoulder blades and into my collarbone. The blood has pooled in my extremities, and my feet are throbbing icebergs. This pain, mixed with my earnest if not raw gratitude, has taken an emotional toll on me. I am full but spent.

Leo finishes packing just as the last credit rolls. We turn to leave, but the lights don't come up. There is a moment of stillness; then I hear my voice echoing again in the theater. To leave now would be noticeable, a scene. I look up to stop Leo, and he turns me back to the screen. As he does, my face fills it. I know this clip. These are my closing remarks, remarks I prepared for an after-party, not as an epilogue to the film. But here it is, embedded just after the credits. Present in the moment, I let my own confession wash over me.

Just one more story.

I was attending my first ALS clinic to learn about all the resources available for people like me. I was surrounded by others, all at varying stages of progression. Knowing intellectually about this horrible disease does nothing to cushion the blow of seeing people totally paralyzed from head to toe with mostly hopeless expressions covering their faces. It was almost more than I could stand. To swallow the truth of your diagnosis is hard. But to witness your future? That was horrifying to me. My instinctive reaction was to say, "Please, please, dear Lord, do not let this happen to me. Do not let me just exist like this."

My greatest fear was to just exist.

But that was then. This is now. Many years have passed, fifteen, to be exact, and today is my turn to be paralyzed from head to toe, relying on machines for every breath, totally dependent upon others. My life today is far from mere existence. See, the presence of God is what produces abundant living, and it is far greater than anything ALS could dish out or negative circumstances could ever produce in your life. I count it true joy in living my life's purpose, which is helping others to know and walk closer with God. That's real living.

I want to personally thank each of you for coming tonight and listening to my story about my God. All my love . . .

Ah, yes. Abundant living—that's the stuff of intimacy. That's the fruit.

The lights come up, and there is a moment of silence. A sound begins to fall like light rain. The crowd is clapping. It is soft at first, then it grows. It grows to what some might call applause, and I look around and see these people standing to their feet. The old John Paine, the one who sought validation in so many other places, the one who didn't understand wholehearted intimacy, would have wanted to sit in this applause,

184

maybe even raise a hand in feigned humility. The new John Paine—the true one—can't. It is past time. I have to escape this fire.

Leo turns me toward the door, takes the ventilator out of my nose, and puts the joystick in my mouth. I push forward, move as fast as the chair will carry me, even as the ovation continues. We push through the doors, and I ask Leo what time it is.

"Eight thirty," he says.

It'll be another hour before I arrive home, and I still have so much to do before my night is over. We'll do the whole dressing routine in reverse; then, when my body is in bed, we'll make our way through the rest of the two-hour ritual. All this pain, this time, this effort—I pray it was worth it.

Could you change just a few people? I ask again. I can sense my friend, Christ, smiling.

We make our way to the elevator, then down to the main lobby. It is empty at first, but by the time we get to the garage elevator, a small crowd has gathered. There is a line, and everyone offers to let me break ranks.

Boy, my butt hurts.

I am in my gown, lying in bed, sequential compression sleeves on my feet. These sleeves do what everyday muscle movement would otherwise accomplish: recirculate the blood pooled in my extremities. Air inflates the toe of the sleeve and pushes the blood into my feet. Then, air fills the foot, then the ankle, then the calf, and as the blood makes its way back to the main circulatory paths, my feet begin to warm.

My BiPAP is in, breathing in rhythm, and the night caretaker is by my bed. He gives me my nightly cocktail—antibiotics, pain medication, medicines to improve my circulation. He asks me about the night, and I smile, tell him it was good—that is my hope, anyway. Exhausted, this is all I can muster. I close my eyes.

The machines that keep me alive whizz, whir, buzz, and gasp. The sounds are rhythmic, though. Gentle. I sit in the cadence, quiet, grateful.

I consider again the tug of this disease, the way it pulls me down, then lets go, then pulls a little further, then lets go again, then pulls yet again. For fifteen years, this has been my life, and one day soon, the disease will pull me to my final breath. The ghost of Lou Gehrig will come with his death grip in those hours, and he will not let go until I'm released into eternity.

Old Lou. Who knew how kindred we'd become?

This rhythm of suffering has worked its miracle in my life. It is the miracle of intimacy only God could have produced, a oneness with his presence. And these are the daily rhythms of that miraculous intimacy: dismiss the God of anger, perfection, and judgment; embrace the God of unconditional love; rest in that love, even in your pain; allow that love to wash over you, to validate you; become more vulnerable to it, trust it—sleep, rise, and start again.

And again.

And again.

I've been asked what I'd do to be rid of this disease. I'm not sure how to answer the question, but let me say it this way: if I could hold Margaret one more time, if I could bounce my grandchildren on my lap or hug my children, if I could put in a full day at the office, if I could be a captain of industry, if I could lead thousands into professions of faith, if I could be the pillar of the church—if I could do it all but had to trade this rhythm of intimacy with God born from ALS? The choice is easy. I would keep this disease. I'd take this pain, this slow suffocation. I'd drink this cup all over again. I wouldn't trade this intimacy for anything. What was meant for my torture has been used for my salvation. I'm thankful for that.

The night is coming, closing in around me. The pain releases as my eyes grow heavy, as I linger between waking and dreaming. I can feel the tug into that other world. Perhaps this is the night I will meet my Jesus. Maybe not. Either way, he is here, my friend, my comfort.

And even in this, I am content.

You guide me with your counsel, and afterward you will take me into glory. Whom have I in heaven but you? And earth has nothing I desire besides you. My flesh and my heart may fail, but God is the strength of my heart and my portion forever. . . . But as for me, it is good to be near God. I have made the Sovereign LORD my refuge; I will tell of all your deeds.

—PSALM 73:24–26, 28

Acknowledgments

To my agent, Sealy Yates, for believing in this message and never giving up. You are a true visionary.

To Margaret and Hillary Paine for allowing me to share some of the harder parts of their lives with the world.

To Gary Wood and A. C. Musgraves, my business partners, friends, and brothers. Thank you for encouraging me to share this message, and to Gary for being a tireless sounding board for this project.

To Seth Haines, the greatest contributor to this project.

To God, for choosing to use the least talented of communicators to deliver his message.

About the Author

J ohn Paine is a successful businessman and lay leader living in Plano, Texas. He has lived more than seventeen years with ALS, also known as Lou Gehrig's disease. A once-active man, John now spends his days in a wheelchair, dependent on a ventilator for his next breath. His greatest passion is mentoring others and sharing the true treasure of his life with them—intimacy with Christ. In the twilight of his life, John most enjoys spending time with his wife, Margaret, and the families of his four adult children and seven grandchildren, and considers himself to be the luckiest man alive.

He passed May 12, 2021

From The Creators Of: *Travis: A Soldier's Story*

THE LUCKIEST MAN

OFFICIAL SELECTION
LIFE FEST
FILM FESTIVAL
HOME OF THE
CAPRA AWARDS
2016

A ⬡ FOTOLANTHROPY FILM

AN INSPIRING TRUE STORY

Don't wait until you are dying before you start living.

FOTOMEDIA GROUP   JOHN PAINE   MARGARET PAINE   JOHN PAINE II   JOSH PAINE   four story creative
WWW.FOTOLANTHROPY.COM   AMANDA WILSON   HILLARY BARKER   DR. JEFFREY ELLIOTT   LEO GARCIA   #LUCKIESTMANFILM

You've experienced the book,
now experience the documentary.

fotolanthropy.com/luckiestmanfilm